The

Road Map

A practical guide for
navigating your way to good credit

BY PATRICK RITCHIE

Success Road Map Press L.L.C.
Chandler, AZ

Success Road Map Press L.L.C.   Mailing Address:
523 W. Knox Road   P.O. Box 12285
Chandler, AZ 85225   Tempe, AZ 85284

Cover Design by Visage Creative Business Services, Inc.
www.visagecreative.com

Editing by Christina McAllister
Editor@SuccessRoadMapPress.com

Photography by Peggy Erickson
www.PeggyEricksonPhotography.com

www.TheCreditRoadMap.com

Library of Congress Number Pending

ISBN 10: 0-9778699-0-3
ISBN 13: 978-0977869909

"But if the test of a subject's historical importance is the amount of controversy it generated, then consumer credit is one of the most significant subjects in the history of the American twentieth century." - *Lendol Calder, Author of "Financing the American Dream: A Cultural History of Consumer Credit" annual credit Report.com*

Table of Contents

Dedication

To my parents, thank you for making me believe there are no limits in life. Thank you to my mother for waking up early and driving me to the golf course every summer so I could caddy. Caddying gave me friends and experiences that never could have otherwise been realized. Thank you to my father for demonstrating to me a strong work ethic, without which this book never could have been written.

About the Author

Patrick Ritchie is an approved instructor with the Arizona Department of Real Estate and owns the Ritchie School of Real Estate Finance in Chandler, AZ. Patrick is a guest speaker for the Ohio State University and Arizona State University Colleges of Business as well as an instructor at Scottsdale Community College. He serves as a member of the USA Today Small Business Panel and is a former Evans Scholar. Patrick is a certified Guerrilla Marketing Coach, based on the best selling *Guerrilla Marketing* titles. His book, *The Credit Road Map*, is required reading in finance and real estate classes at major universities throughout the country.

Patrick has appeared nationally on radio and television to share information about credit and real estate finance. He has taught thousands of people about how the credit system works. Working in the banking industry, Patrick has personally reviewed thousands of credit reports which enables him to provide first-hand knowledge about how lenders view credit. He can be reached via email at Patrick@TheCreditRoadMap.com.

Acknowledgements

This book is the result of every client and every class attendee I have ever had. Each unique credit situation allowed me to see a little bit more of what consumers face on the road to credit greatness.

My Editor and friend, Tina McAllister, blazed the book writing trail as I watched her write and publish her first book. Thank you for showing me the way and encouraging me to sit down to tell the credit story.

My Office Manager, Crystal Myers, has always been there keeping the business moving forward. Her abilities allowed me the opportunity to run a business and write a book at the same time.

Charlie Marsh played a key role in making this book possible. Pushing each other forward as we wrote our books kept me on track.

Mary Dougherty of Bootstrap Publishing helped me tremendously as I learned what it took to write a book. Thank you, Mary!

Someone I cannot thank enough is Craig Watts of Fair Isaac for taking the time to review and provide feedback on some of the most important sections of this book. Your insight is greatly appreciated.

Introduction

"An archer cannot hit the bull's-eye if he doesn't know where the target is." - *Anonymous*

Road Map: a: a detailed plan to guide progress toward a goal. b: a detailed explanation

The purpose of this book is to explain a subject that most people do not fully know or understand. Many people seem to know something about credit, but few know all the information necessary to control their credit. This is your detailed plan to progress toward high credit scores. In return, high credit scores save time, money and energy.

So what does this book offer you?

For those with average credit:
- Some new insight on how you can get your scores higher and stay on the road to financial success.
- Gain an understanding of what is keeping you from having exceptional credit.
- Learn how to redirect your actions to reap the rewards great credit will give you.

For those with less than desirable credit:
- A new way of thinking to get you on the road to financial recovery.
- Ways to overcome negatives, deal with charge-offs and collections.
- Information that will help you identify the circumstances that have hindered you in the past.

For those with above average credit:

- Find out how you got there and more importantly how you can stay there.
- Understand the benefits of always trying to make your credit better, even when you have already achieved excellence.
- Hear the stories of the most common pitfalls those with great credit face and how to protect yourself.

The book has been written in detail to cover the rules of the credit game. I recommend you reading the book in its entirety. But for those who like just the meat and not the potatoes, then look for the re-caps at the end of each chapter and the other icons to identify key points.

Here are the icons you'll want to keep a look out for:

 A key point

 Information you may find useful

 An interesting anecdote, story or example

 Recap at the end of a chapter

Let's face it. Great credit makes life easier. When you finish this book you will know how to take charge of your credit. You will understand the why and the how. Why? You want to pay less to borrow money. You want the best terms and options that lending has to offer. You want to wear your good credit as a badge of honor in front of all who will see it (and thanks to the Fair Credit Reporting Act, not everyone can see it).

So sit down and buckle in for the ride. It may get a bit bumpy along the way, but the destination is worth it!

Chapter 1

Credit: The Foundation of Borrowing

"We are what we repeatedly do. Excellence then, is not an act, but a habit." - *Aristotle*

Without credit the American Dream would be in jeopardy.

A little dramatic, I know. But think about that statement.

Credit is critical to our economy, as critical as gasoline is to making our country function daily. Imagine if there was no gasoline available tomorrow. Our country and our economy would come to a grinding halt.

Now imagine if credit were shut off tomorrow. What would happen? How would you buy a house? A car? How would you afford to go to college? Are you starting to get the picture?

Newsflash: Credit is integral to our lives.

A Credit Test?
Think about it. Most things in life require instruction. In fact, many things require a test! When you wanted to get

your driver's license you had to pass a written test. Then you were allowed to start learning how to drive on the streets. After so many hours of supervised driving, you had your driving test. Some of us may have had to take the driving test more than once to pass, but it made us a safer driver once we were able to pass the test.

What if no tests were required for driving a car and getting that license? How safe would our streets be? We'd have people crossing lanes, driving the wrong direction, ignoring traffic signals. It would be chaotic! That's sort of what it's like with credit. We were turned loose with no instruction. There was no test to pass or fail. Sure, most of us are functioning without issue. Maybe we had a few "accidents" with our credit. But for the most part we steer in the right direction. It's possible to operate a vehicle without really knowing the laws. However, not knowing the laws is what gets us into trouble.

One typical assumption with credit is that as long as we are paying our bills on time our credit must be good. This is partially correct. Paying things on time is a major component to the credit scoring system. Of course there are many other parts that make the credit scoring engine run. You could spend your entire life paying things on time and would likely always have a decent to average credit score. Why not a <u>perfect</u> credit score? Go back to driving a car and compare the act of driving to paying your bills on time. When you are driving you still need to know when to stop, yield, pull to the side for emergency vehicles, keep an eye on your speed, and so on. Credit works the same way. You have to know your credit limits, current balances, etc. You need to know how certain things may affect you. There are numerous things that will affect your credit, not just your timing in paying bills.

We can jeopardize our credit any given day with any number of things. We have to realize the importance our credit has in our lives. Acknowledging this importance can have a major impact on our daily decisions, and in the end, our credit.

Credit Strength = More Possibilities

In a mortgage lending decision the lender will typically look at the credit, income, assets and down payment. It is desirable to be strong in all four and generally sufficient to be strong in two areas. However, if you're only going to be strong in one, hopefully it's credit. Credit will trump income, down payment and assets in many cases. Someone who has strong credit has displayed they are able to manage repaying debt. If you are trying to buy a house and you have an established credit record with high scores there will almost always be options. Even if you have no job or money, there is still a way to get a mortgage. That is how important credit is, it opens up possibilities that are only available to people with great credit.

Good Debt vs. Bad Debt

Two kinds of debt exist: good debt and bad debt. A house or an education are examples of good debt. A house has tax advantages and will go up in value. With education you are expanding your earning potential and hopefully making a return on your investment. Statistics have shown that someone with a college degree will make $1,000,000 more in their lifetime than they would have with just a high school diploma.

The benefits to good debt? Good debt opens up the door to future benefits. Most homeowners enjoy appreciation on their homes that allow them to move up to a larger home at a later point. People who wish to invest in real estate will

16

find that leveraging money through a mortgage is a good way to accumulate properties. In order to do this your credit has to be in good standing. Once you get started you are able to keep moving further up the ladder, whether it is acquiring multiple properties, buying a larger home, or both.

Bad debt has no intrinsic future value. Examples include going out to eat, or seeing a movie. Financing these activities will often lead to paying many times more than the original cost. Most of us have probably charged these things on our credit cards at some point or another. But when that bill comes, what do you do? Paying it in full is the best approach. If you carry the balance and only pay the minimum, beware of the snowball effect. That balance will keep accruing and your ability to borrow money diminishes. So now you're moving in the direction opposite of prosperity. The more bad debt you incur that has no returning value, the further away we move from qualifying for the "good debts" that will allow you to invest in your future.

Federal Trade Commission

The Federal Trade Commission (FTC) works for the consumer to prevent fraudulent, deceptive, and unfair business practices in the marketplace. It provides information to help consumers avoid the unsavory aspects of commerce. The FTC also enforces legislation and investigates complaints made by consumers and consumer advocates. Ensuring that the nation's markets operate efficiently and free of harmful restrictions to consumers is a massive undertaking.

The FTC plays a crucial role in the credit world as both an enforcer of the laws, and a source of answers. The FTC maintains a website that provides educational information on credit reporting and other financial topics affecting consumers. The FTC can be contacted via telephone or email to field complaints and questions consumers have. The U.S. Government Accountability Office published a survey in 2005 that indicated only 6% of respondents knew the FTC is the federal agency they would contact to file a complaint against a credit reporting agency. Of the respondents, 24% answered that they thought the Better Business Bureau was the main point of contact, while 62% answered they did not know. Which group were you in before you read this book?

Fair Isaac

You've probably heard of the Fair Isaac Corporation because it is the creator of the FICO® score. This is the most commonly accepted credit scoring model on the market. But there's a little more to the story.

In 1956, Engineer Bill Fair and mathematician Earl Isaac founded Fair Isaac on an initial investment of $400 each. These guys were way ahead of their time. By 1958 they began building credit scoring systems. Think about the technology back then. A computer was the size of a living room.

By 1991 FICO® scores became available from all three major U.S. credit reporting agencies. This was the start of a new age in lending. In 1995 Fannie Mae and Freddie Mac recommended that mortgage lenders begin using FICO® scores for deciding U.S. mortgage loans. FICO® became the Kleenex® or Coca-Cola® of the credit scoring industry. A name brand that everyone uses to describe a product is something every business with a product dreams about.

Today, Fair Isaac Corporation is the leading provider of decision management solutions powered by advanced analytics. That's a mouthful.

How does analytic decision making work?

1. Start with data, past and current information.

2. Explore and analyze the data. Find patterns that help solve the problem and guide decisions.

3. Write equations that map present data to future performance, and actions to results. Develop the decision strategy that solves the problem.

4. Wire the enterprise for consistent real-time decisions, with software that embeds analytics and strategies within business processes.

Sound simple? Remember when you were sitting in math class and inevitably someone always asked "When am I ever going to use this?" At Fair Isaac they do math that will make the average person's brain melt. These are the people who paid attention and are now putting that knowledge to good use.

What does all of this math ultimately accomplish?
- Reduced operating costs
- Broader customer base
- Speedier decisions
- Growth in customer value
- Increased revenues
- Diminished losses

Sure, you probably don't care about any increase in customer base or reduction of operating costs. But it means a lot to the companies that extend credit to you. They want to know that financing your home or car (insert your dream purchase here) isn't going to cost them an arm and a leg. They want to make sure you're a "good" risk.

Want to check out your score? By going to www.myFICO.com, consumers can purchase their scores. The website is full of great information on credit.

An Early Start...

The rite of passage into adulthood no longer seems to be the ability to vote at age 18. It seems to have been surpassed by receiving your first credit card. And it's not too surprising that so many teens jump on the credit bandwagon early. Millions of dollars are poured into marketing credit cards to high school and college students. USA Today notes that Citibank, the largest issuer of Visa, may spend $10 million in a single year just marketing credit cards to high school and college students. And of course college campuses have no problem allowing access to the students. Colleges can earn $50,000 to $100,000 per year just by allowing a credit card company to operate on campus.

I remember how I felt when I received my first credit card. When I first received the credit card I felt empowered. There I was a college freshman with a $3,000 credit limit. Then I became a college sophomore with $3,000 of credit card debt. I felt like I had been punched in the stomach. Oh, there are plenty of fond memories of what I spent the $3,000 on. Let's see, there were great movies, dinners, CD's, electronics, basically nothing that I still have in my possession. Although I must confess that I did not use the entire limit on frivolous items. I used $2,000 of it to start a side business aerating lawns. Basically my first loan in the business world was my credit card. Fortunately I made enough on that venture to pay back the debt.

According to USA Today the typical credit card holder has seven cards with an average balance of $1,642. That would mean the average credit card holder has over $11,000 in credit card debt.

***

How it All Began

The first use of credit cards in the United States dates back to the 1920's. Oil companies and hotel chains began issuing credit to customers. In 1946 the first bank issued credit card to be used among numerous merchants came from Flatbush National Bank of Brooklyn. John Biggins, the inspiration behind the idea, created the "Charge-It" card for use between bank clients and the local merchants.

On a nationwide scale, Frank McNamara was one of the pioneers of the credit card industry. He was the creator of the Diners Club Card. In 1949 McNamara had a business dinner at a New York restaurant. Forgetting his cash in his other suit he was in the awkward position of not being able to pay for dinner. The embarrassment brought on McNamara's idea. "Why should people be limited to spending what they have in cash as opposed to what they can afford?" In early 1950 McNamara went back to the same restaurant with his business partner, Ralph Schneider. At the end of dinner McNamara presented a card and was able to sign for the purchase. This is known as the First Supper in the credit card industry.

By 1958 both American Express and Bank of America issued their first credit cards. The BankAmericard is known more commonly today as Visa. In 1966, Interbank Card Association was started and is known today as MasterCard International. Both Visa and MasterCard acted as centralized payment systems for member banks.

Initially credit cards were meant for travelers, primarily traveling sales people and business executives. As more companies began to offer credit cards the promotions changed to a time-saving device for everyone, not just travelers.

Catchy Advertising

Credit card companies spend a lot of money to get us to use their cards. Their slogans are some of the most memorable advertising out there.

- American Express: Don't leave home without it.
- Discover Card: It pays to Discover.
- MasterCard: There are some things money can't buy. For everything else there's MasterCard.
- Visa: It's everywhere you want to be.
- Capital One: What's in your wallet?

The Priceless® Campaign

The MasterCard Priceless® advertising campaign was launched in October 1997 and has arguably been the most successful advertising campaign ever launched by a financial service company. The campaign has earned major creative awards and more than 100 individual awards.

The priceless moment always occurs after a series of purchases are made. MasterCard is touching the emotional nature of consumerism. Your first date with your future spouse may be priceless, but it still costs money to go out on a date. Hey, spending money and your happiness go hand in hand, right?

MasterCard International is the owner of U.S. service mark registration for the mark "PRICELESS" and they guard that term zealously. In fact, attorneys for MasterCard have sent legal correspondence to people who host websites containing parodies of the Priceless commercial. The parodies in question range from obscene to political and have been making the rounds via email for years. It seems like almost everyone with Photoshop has made an attempt at humor at the expense of MasterCard. This just shows the homerun MasterCard hit with this campaign. Imitation is the best form of flattery, right?

In August 2000 MasterCard filed a $5 million lawsuit against Ralph Nader and his Campaign Committee for using the priceless concept for a campaign ad. MasterCard claimed that the ads were an infringement of copyright and trademark laws. The campaign ad took the same format as the MasterCard commercials. A voice states, "Grilled tenderloin for fund raiser: $1,000 a plate. Campaign ads filled with half truths: $10 million. Promises to special interest groups: over $10 billion. Finding out the truth: Priceless. There are some things money can't buy. Without Ralph Nader in the presidential debates, the truth will come in last."

In March 2004 a trial court ruled in favor of Nader by ruling the use was fair.

Welcome to the World of Centurion®...

In 1984 a rumor started that the "elite of the elite" were issued a black American Express Card that enabled them to buy anything. A 1988 article in *The Wall Street Journal* confirmed the existence of a black American Express Card used for identification for large sum check cashing. Leveraging the allure of this mysterious black card, American Express introduced the Centurion® Card in 1999. The card is reserved exclusively for the chosen few existing American Express customers who have displayed enormous buying power. It cannot be applied for; the Centurion® Card is by invitation only.

The American Express website has very little information about the Centurion® Card other than acknowledging its existence. Published information regarding the card indicates the annual fee to be $2,500. I couldn't get past the first page of www.centurioncard.com without a login and password, such is the secretive nature of this elite card. I had to dig deeper, so I turned to eBay. On eBay I was able to purchase "The Centurion® Card Welcome Kit" being sold as a rare collector's item. Now I have access to a 38 page hardbound book detailing all the benefits the card provides. It is impressive; the inside of the book is black velvet with two slots where the cards are held. The book outlines everything a card holder can expect.

A letter inside the front cover of the book starts out, "Welcome to Centurion: The most sought-after American Express card in the world." It goes on to describe how a dedicated team of professionals will help the card holder enjoy enhanced levels of luxury and comfort, 24 hours a day, 365 days a year.

One call can arrange:
- Japanese orchids flown in for your daughter's wedding
- A hard to come by table at a top restaurant
- Hiring your own private jet
- Scuba diving lessons in the Red Sea, and to confirm your insurance covers you

- Referral to an English-speaking doctor or lawyer anywhere in the world 24 hours a day
- Your social events or obtain "hard to come by" tickets to events around the world
- No extra cost for room upgrades and late check-out
- Unrestricted access to the world's largest network of over 400 airport lounges at all major locations worldwide
- Shopping with a pre-arranged private shopping assistant, home delivery, private viewing or shopping events
- Your ideal vacation destination

Not to mention the insurance coverage that comes with the card:

Missed Departure: $870
Medical Expenses: $8,000,000
Baggage Delay: $350 after 12 hours

Supposedly the latest round of Centurion® Cards are made of titanium instead of plastic. Perhaps this provides the added protection of deflecting a bullet.

- Credit is critical to our economy. Without credit, we would have trouble buying cars, homes, affording an education. And the list goes on. Credit isn't bad...we just have to make sure we know the rules of credit in order for it to work <u>for</u> us, rather than against us.
- There is an actual dollar value attached to having good credit. A person with bad or below average credit will pay more for things than their neighbor with good credit. So by having better credit you can <u>save</u> money!

- Good credit is more than just paying bills on time. Many daily decisions affect your credit in ways you may not even realize.
- There is a difference in debt. There's the "good debt" and the "bad debt." The good stuff gives you a return on your investment, like a house or an education. The bad stuff is when you use credit for things like dinner, movies, that extra humongous television for the family room. And if you don't pay that bad debt off, it will keep snowballing into a balance that negatively affects your credit scores and impacts your life for years to come.
- The Federal Trade Commission (FTC) is your friend. It looks out for consumers to ensure credit reports are factual and that you have not fallen victim to unfair business practices.
- Fair Isaac is the company that created the FICO® score – the score that has become all too important in our credit lives. A lot of mathematical, analytical mumbo-jumbo is what has created this number that creates a major impact on our ability to get that "good debt."

***

C hapter 2

Rules to Credit Scores

"If winning isn't everything, why do they keep score?"
- Vince Lombardi

Since credit is the measure for our cost to borrow, it is important to know how to maneuver through the tangled web of credit. There are rules involved and the problem with these rules is that nobody ever handed us a slip of paper with the rules all spelled out. You may have learned how to balance a checkbook at some point in your education, but managing credit is not something you find in our financial curriculum. How can you successfully play a game and win if you were never given the rules of the game? Knowing the rules of the game is just as important as the ability to play the game. Think of it in terms of driving. If you run a red light, you can get a ticket. Drive faster than the speed limit, you'll get a ticket. It's the same in the world of credit. If you misstep, you can lose ground (i.e. your credit scores go down). It could be a minor loss or a substantial loss depending on whether you are making any major purchases in the near future. And there are a lot more people watching your credit than watching the roads.

The last time you went for a test drive was your credit report obtained by the dealership without your permission? This is an issue that has been addressed by the Federal Trade Commission in an advisory letter dated February 1998 to the Texas Automobile Dealers Association. The FTC said, "An automobile dealer may obtain a [credit] report only in those circumstances in which the consumer clearly understands that he or she is initiating the purchase or lease of a vehicle and the seller has a legitimate business need for the consumer report to complete the transaction." The act of test driving does not initiate a business transaction. The dealer should obtain written permission to check a credit report before or during a test drive. Reputable dealerships will not check a consumer's credit report without asking. However, it is a good idea to find out the dealership's policy before going for a test drive. Having your credit report checked by a dealership is not a big deal; in fact, if you are going to be financing your purchase it is necessary. Having a credit check performed every weekend is not a good thing since there is a degree of credit score decline from credit inquiries. This is would be more of a concern for someone who regularly test drives cars as a hobby.

***

The good news is that you can change your credit scores on your own at any point. Will it happen overnight? Not likely. There are numerous variables that go into determining your scores. However, these variables will be identified so you can figure out what will help you the most with your current situation.

Cynthia had a 550 credit score 3 years ago. Today she has a 750 middle score because she followed the rules of credit. What does that mean in terms of dollars? When she *financed a car for $20,000 on a five year term she got a rate of 5%. Cynthia's payment is $377.42. If her score had stayed at 550, that rate would likely be 9% or more. With a 9% rate, the payment would have been $415.17. The difference is $37.75 per month, $452.97 per year, and $2,264.83 for the five year loan term. By cleaning up her score, Cynthia was able to save quite a bit of money.*

What could you do with an extra $2,264.83? Pay off existing debts? Put it toward retirement? We rarely look at things in terms of small pieces, but these small pieces become larger over time. In fact, if you increase the interest rate by 1% on every loan the average consumer has it would equal over $54,000 extra paid out over a 30 year period. In the same sense, subtracting 1% would be a savings of $54,000 over the next 30 years. We're talking about the equivalent of an annual salary.

Now we can see the true dollar value when we know the rules of credit.

Look at the things that we finance. It really does add up. Car loans, credit cards, mortgage payments, student loans; we finance many things that we need. And in some cases we finance things that we <u>don't</u> need.

Whatever the case may be, you can't play the game if you don't know the rules. And you certainly can't expect to win the game. So learning the rules of credit will not only help you play that game, but hopefully enable you to win the game and get control of your financial life!

There are two sets of rules: one involves how your credit score is determined and the other involves the laws that govern reporting. We will look at the Fair Credit Reporting Act in a future chapter. It's more important for you as a consumer to first know how credit scores work before getting into the laws regarding credit reporting. Once we know how the scoring works then we can use the laws to our benefit.

Did you know that credit scores are not a part of the credit report? The score is a *product* sold with a credit report. And what is the score exactly? It is a three digit number that indicates how likely a consumer is to repay debt. The credit score can determine whether we will be granted credit, like it or not, in a variety of circumstances. When we are granted credit, the credit score will often influence what our interest rate and down payment will be, along with a few other factors.

The score is developed based on the information contained in the credit report. The higher the credit score, the better. The Fair Isaac Corporation, creator of the FICO® score, has published a scoring range of 300 - 850. Other scoring models may differ slightly, but the range published by Fair Isaac is what we will consider since it is the most popular scoring model.

When we were in school many of us used our grades to measure our status in the class. It told us where we stood and how we were performing. In the real world, our credit scores are our closest measure to "grades." Credit scores tell us where we stand and how we are performing in the world of borrowing and repaying money. However, it goes beyond money. Your credit may help determine your employment or where you live. Many large employers look at credit before making a hiring decision. Landlords look at credit before making the decision to rent. Banks, employers, and landlords look at credit history as a measure of character and our willingness to repay.

So what kind of scores do lenders look for? From a mortgage lending perspective all consumers should shoot for a credit score of 720 or higher. This will generally put a person in the best position to get the best available terms for a lending product. Obviously there are other considerations such as income, down payment, etc. However, the scores themselves have a major impact on the approval, especially automated approvals where a computer program is making the decision. One benefit may be that a person with high credit scores is approved for a mortgage based on the high credit scores and now does not have to provide actual evidence of income (pay stubs and W2's), just verification they are currently employed (a telephone call to the employer). A score of 660 - 719 is still respectable and will likely result in favorable terms in most cases. A consumer should always try to be above 600 - 659 as this range is getting close to what would likely cause a greater increase in interest rate. A score of 599 or below is generally going to be considered low and will in most cases result in less favorable terms (higher interest rate, larger down payment, possibly more fees and conditions) for a consumer.

The median FICO® score is approximately 723.

***

And guess what? You don't have just one score. You have three! Experian, Equifax, and TransUnion all provide a credit score to lenders as a separate product from the credit report (consumers have to request a score specifically and pay for it). In fact, lenders usually get all three reports "bundled" into one, rather than having to request each one separately as consumers typically do. This is commonly referred to as a tri-merge credit report. The three scores usually differ from one another. A mortgage lender will often use the middle of the three scores when making a lending decision. Here's an example:

Gwen applies for a loan and the lender obtains her scores of 724, 735, and 756. The lender will use the middle score of 735 as the credit score used in making a lending decision.

But what if one of the bureaus doesn't have enough information to produce a score? If a consumer has minimal amounts of credit, she may only have two scores to look at.

Gwen only has two scores, a 724 and a 756. The lender will use the lower of the two scores, rather than averaging the two together. So to the lender, Gwen has a credit score of 724.

Each credit bureau has a slightly different equation for how the scores are determined. For the most part you will only see a large difference when one or two of the credit reports is missing information or contains incorrect information. For example:

Bob applies for a loan and his scores come back at 598, 678 and 697. His middle score would be 678, but why such a difference in the three scores? Bob disputed an error on his credit report that was hurting his scores but he didn't follow up to make sure all three bureaus made the correction.

This is pretty common. Many consumers forget to dispute with all three of the credit bureaus. Make sure you always dispute items with all three of the credit bureaus. Another possibility?

Bob has a collection account that was only reported to one credit bureau. Two bureaus never received this negative information and therefore his scores with them remained higher.

Though rare, this does happen. In Bob's situation the vast difference in scores really did not hurt him since he had two strong scores. In some situations positive credit history may only be reported to one or two of the bureaus. If a bureau is missing positive information it could result in a lower score.

We tend to speak in threes when it comes to credit. Yet, there are mortgage lenders that only look for one credit bureau score. For instance, I have worked with lenders that only use the score provided by Experian. Others use the score provided by TransUnion exclusively. A rare occurrence is when a lender averages the three scores and uses the result as the score (I know of only one lender using this method currently). This is unique and is a small percentage of overall mortgage lending. However, it does illustrate the point that we always want to take care of all three scores.

Tim has scores of 560, 697, and 729 and the lender only considers his TransUnion score. The 560 came from TransUnion. Unfortunately it is his worst score and he will likely be turned down for the loan, unless he has a substantial down payment. The cause of the 560 score could have been an error. Therefore Tim will need to look at his three credit reports to determine the differences. Once he is able to identify the differences he can address the cause of the lower credit score.

Having three scores that vary greatly indicates there is something being reported that the three bureaus do not share in common. Something could be missing or incorrect in his credit report. A common culprit would be judgments and tax liens. In the mortgage industry we observe many cases where a public record is reporting differently among the three credit bureaus. Tim may also want to shop around. Another lender might look at a different report and make a different lending decision.

Is there great disparity between your three credit scores? Here are some causes of variation among the three credit scores:

1. In some cases information is reported to a particular bureau quicker and will reflect on the other reports at a later point.
2. A disputed item is corrected, but was never disputed with the other bureau(s), or was not corrected by the other bureau(s).
3. All three scoring models are slightly different and will typically have a small spread between them.

In general we see the slight difference in the credit scores because credit reporting agencies organize consumer data differently. This difference makes it impossible for all three credit bureaus to use the same algorithm.

***

Despite the fact that a higher credit score is better, it does not always reign supreme. For example, with Federal Housing Administration (FHA) loans there is no reward for having a higher credit score. A buyer with a 720 and a buyer with a 580 would likely get the same interest rate on a FHA loan (even a buyer with no credit score would get the same rate on a FHA loan). The reason? Your typical mortgage qualification is based on more than just the credit score. A higher credit score is going to make it easier than a lower credit score to qualify you for a loan. However, there are other things taken into consideration such as income, debt-to-income ratio, assets/reserves, overall condition of the credit, etc. You'll find an entire section of the book dedicated to these circumstances.

The bottom line is that higher is better when it comes to credit scores. Although it is just as important to realize that a lower score is not the end of the world. Our objective is to identify the reason the scores are not as high as they could be and fix it to maximize those scores.

The Five Sacred Factors

"If you don't know where you are going, you will wind up somewhere else." - Yogi Berra

Now we look at how those scores come to be. In the lending industry there are fives areas that impact the credit scores. Keep in mind that to generate a credit score there typically needs to be at least one account that has been open for six months or longer. On the same note there must be at least one account with activity reported within the past six months.

1) Payment history accounts for 35% of the score. Paying accounts on-time is the largest factor for credit scores. An account is considered on-time for reporting purposes as long as the payment is received within 30 days of the due date. If you sent out your payment one day past the due date it may be late in the eyes of the lender. You could be subject to a late charge, but if it is received before it is 30 days past due it will not affect your credit scores. I have had several clients who were nervous about late payments only to find out their credit reports do not reflect any late payments. Could a lender report an account that was one day past due as being late to the credit bureaus? Absolutely. Will they? Not likely. It is an accepted practice by lenders to report only payments that are 30 days late. I have yet to encounter a lender that reports prior to 30 days past due. However, we still want to be accountable by sending our payments in before they are due.

Try not to cut it close when making your payments. One 30 day late payment could cause a significant drop in credit scores. The actual impact varies depending on how much positive credit you already have on the report. Here are a couple examples:

Paul has only two open and active credit card accounts and nothing else. He has had these accounts for two years and has always been on-time. One 30 day late payment could drop his scores dramatically. If he had a 650 credit score, a 30 day late could drop his score to below 600 and put him in the 500's. Without a lot of credit to begin with, it is imperative for Paul to keep his payments on-time since he has a smaller credit history.

Jane has had 5 open and active credit card accounts for over 10 years. She also has a mortgage over 4 years old and a car payment over 3 years old. All of her accounts have always been on-time. One 30 day late will not have as much of a negative effect on her credit scores. If she had an 800 score before a 30 day late payment it might drop her to the low 700's. At 700 Jane still has very good credit. Since she has a long positive credit history Jane is not as worse off with one negative item on her credit report.

2) Balances owed accounts for 30% of the score. The balances we carry have an impact on the credit scores. This comes into play mostly with revolving accounts such as credit cards. The rule of thumb is that you should try to keep your balances on credit cards less than 50% of the available credit limit. Some industry spokespeople have even advised keeping credit card balances under 35% of the available limit. The closer you get to the limit on an account the more likely you are to see a decline in credit scores. Try to keep your credit card balances as low as possible.

Tom applied for a mortgage in October and had a middle credit score of 723. He did not purchase a house until February. A new credit report was requested because a credit report is usually not good after 90 days from the original date it was requested. The new credit report showed a credit score of 679. The drop in score was a surprise to both Tom and the lender. There were no late payments, and he had not received any new credit. The one thing that changed was the amounts of his credit card balances. When Tom applied he had almost no balances on his credit cards. During the holidays he used his credit cards and his balances were now near the available limits. Despite his good credit score previously, the lower score must now be used.

The above scenario happens a lot. And it may or may not affect a mortgage approval. With a standard mortgage it may not make a difference at all. However, if a buyer is using a niche product for a $0 down investment property, this lowered score can be quite detrimental.

In some cases people use their credit cards and pay them off in full each month. Keep in mind that a credit score is a snap shot of the credit report at one moment in time. If you are maxed out at that time you may have a lower score than after you pay the balance in full. This is really important to keep in mind if you know you will be making a large purchase that will require financing in the near future. Another thing to consider is that your credit report could reflect your balance on the previous month, not the current month. If you pay off your balance today it could be 30 days or more until it is reflected on your credit report. It is better to split charges on two or more accounts than to max out one each month.

Set a bar for credit cards. Never go over 50% of the available balance at anytime during the month!
***

Installment loan balances are not as much of a factor when compared to revolving accounts. The balance on an installment loan only goes down. On a revolving account, the balance can go up and down and up again. In fact, on installment loans, once you have paid down 20% of the original balance it is a strong indication that you will repay the debt in full. The biggest influence I have seen is when there are large balance installment loans being reported onto the credit report in a short period of time.

Lily recently graduated from law school and will have approximately $100,000 in student loans becoming payable soon. Lily just bought a house and a new car within the past year and did not have any previous credit history. With this large amount of installment debt on her record, Lily's scores are around 620. She has a perfect payment history, but the amount of installment debt coupled with a short credit history has impacted her scores. It will take some time for her balance to fall appreciably and have a less negative effect on her scores.

3) Length of credit history accounts for 15% of the score. The longer positive credit history the better. We can control this to a certain extent. An installment loan has a set lifespan and will be closed when the last payment has been made. Conversely, credit cards (revolving accounts) can have an infinite lifespan. There is one thing I hear people advised to do that makes my skin crawl, "Pay off your credit cards and close them." Contrary to popular belief, closing accounts is not a good thing when it comes to credit scores. If you cannot withstand the temptation to accumulate more debt on open credit cards, then perhaps closing the accounts is your best bet. But I would still recommend putting them out of immediate reach (safe deposit box) to avoid spontaneous purchases and keeping them open if at all possible. You know your habits so do what is right for you.

The length of time open is an important factor in the credit score. Typically anything over seven years old is considered well established. Anything less than three years old can be considered less established, especially the first twelve months an account is open. In between is average. The magic number here is seven years and greater from what I have seen (although Fair Isaac has said there is not a fixed magic number for age when it comes to FICO® scores, simply older is better). This doesn't mean accounts that have aged from four to six years are not important. They are. All open accounts are important because they are aging and positively impacting the credit score as time passes. The bottom line is that age matters when it comes to how long an account we are paying on has been open. You can get there by leaving credit cards open and taking care of them with on-time payments and managing the balances.

The clients I have with 800+ credit scores share a common bond. They have 2 to 10 credit cards that have been open for over seven years. The credit card is the one sure way to get there and stay there. Most installment loans have a much shorter life. Most car loans are anywhere from 2 to 6 years and will never hit the seven year mark. Student loans have a greater chance of getting there, but only after you are finished consolidating. A mortgage may be amortized for 30 years, but the average mortgage is paid off within 5 years. Either the homeowner sells the house or refinances the loan. When you refinance or consolidate you are paying off the old loan and starting a new one. Therefore, credit cards become our one stable friend in the arena of aging accounts.

Often people ask me if a person's age has anything to do with their credit scores. The answer is a firm no (see Equal Credit Opportunity Act). However, depending on one's age they are more likely to have credit cards that have aged to seven years and beyond. But remember, age is not a predictor of credit success. I have had clients who are 25 years old in the 800 range. And I have had older clients with much lower scores.

Credit cards over seven years old put you on the road to a positive credit history. If something negative were to happen at a given point, your longer history will usually prevail. From a lending standpoint we can see if someone has always been reliable by paying their bills on-time. A greater portion of positive credit will withstand a bump in the road.

Think about it. The longer an account is open, the more it conveys about an individual's willingness and ability to make payments as scheduled. New accounts may convey little information other than that a consumer has had a recent need for credit and has been approved for credit.

So what happens when we close our credit card accounts? Closing an account will never improve a person's FICO® score. In fact, it could lower it. The reason for this is credit utilization. Owing the same amount of revolving debt, but having fewer overall accounts with available credit could cause a decline in credit scores. I've heard many people say, "Well, I don't use this card anyway, I might as well just close it out." This is not wise. Having good credit utilization is good for your score. Closing accounts removes available credit without necessarily reducing outstanding debt, which could result in raising the credit utilization ratio. The result of this could be a decline in credit scores. We want the age of our accounts to continue to progress, but it goes beyond just age when you consider the credit utilization factor.

When an account is closed it will at some point not factor into the credit scores at all. It could be years, as this will not occur until the account is completely removed from the credit report by the credit bureaus. Once an account is closed it is put on the path of removal from the credit report at some point in the future. Until complete removal, according to Fair Isaac, old tradelines will continue to have influence on the score.

Just because you keep the credit card accounts open does not mean you have to use them frequently. I try to use mine at least annually so that they do not get closed due to inactivity. When I go on vacation I spread the costs across three cards to keep a lower balance and to show activity.

A 30 day late is not as significant as a 60 day late. However, a 30 day late last month is more significant than a 60 day late five years ago.

***

4) New credit accounts for 10% of the score. Inquiries and new accounts fall into this category. Every time a lender gets your credit report or credit score it shows up as an inquiry on your credit report. An inquiry can have a small impact on your credit score, maybe a decline of a point. Gaining a new credit account can have a larger impact on your credit score in the short term. The main thing is to not apply for unneeded credit.

According to Fair Isaac, any mortgage or auto inquiries posted in the previous 30 days will not affect your FICO® score. In addition, any auto or mortgage inquiries in a 14 day period, within the past year, will be reduced into a single inquiry. In other words, multiple inquiries within a 14 day time frame will show up as only one inquiry. The assumption is that you are pursuing one car loan or one mortgage. Let's face it. You probably won't be buying multiple cars or several homes at a time. But you can get a new credit card with every application. So there is no forgiveness when it comes to applications for credit cards. Therefore every credit card application can result in a decline to your credit score.

Here's how it works...you go to several car dealerships over the weekend and allow each dealership to look at your credit report or credit score. Each look will only count as one inquiry in the scoring model. The same is true for mortgages. The key is to do your shopping for financing in as short a period of time as possible. By doing this you are less likely to cause your credit scores to go down.

Obviously at some point we need to apply for credit. The best way is to spread out purchases enough to where it does not appear you are trying to acquire a lot of credit in a short time frame. Generally credit inquiries only appear on your credit report for 24 months. These inquiries are less detrimental if spread over time.

FICO® scores pay attention to credit inquiries that the consumer initiated by applying for credit, requesting a mortgage quote, or accepting an offer of credit. The scoring model ignores any credit inquiries that are not directly initiated by the consumer. Promotional offers (pre-approved applications) are considered soft inquiries and therefore do not hurt the credit scores. Under such circumstances there is no application for credit on the consumer's part, just information gathering by a direct marketer trying to sell something or lend money. In fact, FICO® scores only consider inquiries within the last 12 months in the score.

There is a rumor that opting out of pre-screened offers will boost a credit score simply because of the elimination of promotional inquiries. This is not true. Promotional inquiries do not factor into the credit score anyway. Eliminating them only reduces the amount of junk mail you will receive, there is no bearing on the credit scores from opting out.

***

5) Mix of credit accounts for 10% of the score. A good mix of credit would be credit cards, car loans, mortgages, student loans, etc. Having a mix of credit is ideal. However, it is not imperative. Over time the credit picture will naturally develop a mix on its own as our needs change. Someone with only credit card accounts and nothing else may be at the most risk. However this is not always the case, and keep in mind the "mix" is only 10% of the overall formula.

Melanie has 8 credit cards with a combined available limit of $80,000. All of the accounts are over 10 years old and have a $0 balance. There are no late payments on the credit report (at least not for the past 7 years). Melanie's middle credit score is 799. Despite the fact that there are *no installment loans and no mix of credit, her scores are still very high.*

I have seen this scenario time and time again. Don't be too concerned about the number of credit cards you have as long as you are managing them well.

Universal Default

Universal default is an interest rate hike triggered by how other credit accounts have been handled. Here are some reasons for universal default rate hikes:

- Credit score has gone down
- Late on an account
- Over credit limit
- High balances on revolving accounts
- Applying for too much credit in short timeframe

Not only can these things trigger a rate increase, but they can also result in a credit limit reduction. This is yet another reason to manage our credit effectively. One poor decision or some form of incorrect negative information can cause a lot of damage beyond just applying for new credit.

Times have certainly changed. The sage advice from the 1960's does not match anything that we need to do today to keep our credit scores healthy. Back then, here's what consumers were told:

- Get a telephone in your name and buy a plane ticket from a major airline.
- Do not buy anything on credit that could be considered frivolous.

- Do all of your grocery shopping at an independent grocery store where you can get to know the owner. Buy "high margin" items such as packaged convenience foods. You will be recognized as a valuable customer. One day forget your wallet and ask to put your groceries on a tab. Pay the tab the same day. Continue putting your groceries on your tab and paying it immediately. The owner will notice and become a good credit reference.
- If you are being interviewed by a credit manager for a credit card do not give the impression that you need it. Make the manager believe you want it for convenience only.

Early forms of credit scores simply listed excellent, good, fair, or poor. The basis of these assigned grades was much different than what we know today as credit scoring. Here are some examples:

- Occupation - Executives, military officers and teachers ranked highest; Lawyers, plumbers and truck drivers ranked in the middle; Musicians, door-to-door salesman and cab drivers ranked the lowest.
- Length of time on current and previous job - seven years was key
- Residence - own, rent, living with parents, renting a room
- Time at present address - over five years was favorable
- Marital status - Married or widowed ranked highest, while a divorced male ranked the lowest
- Weekly earnings
- Bank accounts - Both checking and savings ranked highest, while just a checking and no savings ranked lowest.
- Credit references - Gas and department store cards ranked highest, while finance companies and jewelry store cards ranked lowest.

Although these specific items do not factor into the credit scores, lenders could consider these items individually in qualifying. Some of these items would be especially important when underwriting a loan application for a person without a traditional credit report. It is important to point out that mortgage lenders do not consider the type of occupation, just the length of time in the job. Marital status does not make a difference in qualifying for a mortgage, but could be important to clarify in the case of a community property state.

Source: Al Griffin, *The Credit Jungle* (Chicago: Henry Regnery Company, 1971) pp. 157-160, 165-166.

***

Today's scoring model designed by Fair Isaac is much less biased. FICO® scores ignore:

- Race, color, religion, national origin, sex and marital status
- Age
- Salary, occupation, title, employer, date employed or employment history
- Where you live
- Interest rates you are being charged
- Reported child/family support or rental agreements
- Information not contained in the credit report

Every Seven Years We Can Be Perfect

"Do not let the future be held hostage by the past."
- Neal A. Maxwell

Lending decisions are based on our history of paying back what we borrow. As the saying goes, "History repeats itself." And it often does. The beauty about credit history is that we only have to worry for the most part about the past seven years. This is different in the case of bankruptcies, tax liens, and judgments, which will be discussed in-depth later. The majority of people only have to worry about the previous seven years. For example, let's say Joanne was thirty days late on a credit card payment every month for 12 months. This was eight years ago. Today, Joanne can breathe a sigh of relief because, by Federal law, it's no longer on her credit report since it's been over seven years. If it did appear on her credit report Joanne would be able to have the derogatory history removed.

Seven years is our magic number. You do not have to be perfect for a lifetime to have perfect credit. Here is a breakdown of the various negative information lifespan:

- Late payment (delinquencies) - A late payment is classified as being 30 days, 60 days, 90 days, 120 days, 180 days, etc. A late payment can remain on the credit report for seven years. If someone has a 30 day late payment it will most adversely affect the credit score in the first year. The more time that passes the less impact that 30 day late will have on the credit score. By the sixth year a 30 day late payment will have very little negative impact if the overall credit picture is positive. In the case of a mortgage, never get to 90 - 120 days late. Many mortgage guidelines look at a 90 - 120 day late status as being in foreclosure, even if foreclosure never occurred.

- Charged-off accounts - Typically a credit card that is late past a certain point without payment will become a charge-off. This means the credit card issuer has written off the debt. A charge-off can remain for seven years from the date of the original late payment. If someone was late on 6/1/2000 and never made another payment it would probably reach charge-off status within 120 days. On 6/1/2007 the charge-off would have to come off of the credit report as seven years would have passed since the original derogatory date (the original late payment).

- Collections - Will remain for seven years from the original derogatory date. Most collections are placed from a debt that did not have a specified repayment plan, such as a medical bill. In some circumstances it could be a credit card that was not paid, became a charge-off, and later went into collection by a collection agency. In the case of a medical collection it will remain for seven years from the date the collection was first reported. For a credit card collection or an installment loan collection it would remain for seven years from the original late date. If a collection is paid in full or settled for less (negotiated for a lesser amount than what was originally owed) it will still remain for seven years from the original derogatory date. Showing a zero balance owed is better than having a balance still owed, however, it does not change the length of time it will remain on the credit report.

- Closed accounts - Can remain on the credit report beyond seven years. However, if there were any late payments on the account, the record of those late payments must come off of the credit report once it has been seven years from the time of the late payment. There is a myth that paying off an account and closing it will remove any negative impacts from previously late payments. This is false.

- Judgment - Remains for seven years from the date filed or until the statute of limitations expires, whichever is longer. This includes child support judgments. Once payment has been made on a judgment it is important to verify it is reporting as satisfied (paid). If a judgment is being reported as "not satisfied" then the account shows as being owed and has a more negative impact than if it showed "paid in full" or "satisfied." For old judgments it may be a good idea to contact the court to make a "motion to vacate." This could get the judgment reversed if the consumer can show reason that they were not properly informed (served) of the proceedings. You may want to consult an attorney for legal advice with regards to "motion to vacate" and "service of process" when it comes to attempting to have a judgment removed.

- Bankruptcy - A chapter 7 bankruptcy will remain on the credit report for 10 years from when it was discharged. Lenders generally consider the discharge date in approving loans, not the filing date. There is typically a three month difference from the filing date to the discharge date. A chapter 13 bankruptcy will remain for 7 years from the filing date. A bankruptcy falls into the public record category on the credit report and is separate from the accounts that were included in the bankruptcy. The accounts included in the bankruptcy will remain for seven years from the date they were reported as being included in the bankruptcy.

- Tax liens - Unpaid tax liens can remain forever from the filing date. The Fair Credit Reporting Act gives no time limit for unpaid tax liens. However, the credit bureaus can limit how long they will report unpaid tax liens. For example, Experian will only report unpaid tax liens for 15 years. A paid tax lien will remain seven years from the date paid.

- Inquiries - Most of the time inquiries will show up on the credit report for twelve months. It can remain for up to two years. Consumers see all inquiries on the credit reports they request from the credit bureaus. Pre-approved offers and employment screenings will not show up on a lender's credit report. The reason is that only inquiries triggered by the pursuit of new credit will show up on the credit report a lender purchases to make a lending decision.

- <u>Lost or stolen credit cards</u> - If there is nothing negative such as late payments or a past due amount this is considered neutral information and does not influence the credit score. Although if the lost or stolen credit card had late payments, those specific instances would revert to the seven year rule.

- <u>Positive information</u> – No time limit. Although a closed account with only positive information will likely be removed at some point by the credit bureaus, this timeframe may be in excess of ten years. If you have a closed, positive account on your credit report there is no reason to be concerned about it since it does not have a negative impact.

Keep in mind, creditors reporting to the credit bureaus is voluntary. There are no federal or state laws requiring creditors to report information to the credit reporting agencies. Nor is there anything that requires a creditor to report to all three of the credit bureaus. Also, in the past the format of reporting was not uniform. This has created variations in completeness and frequency in reporting. However, in 2005 a uniform format was required by the credit bureaus for all information submissions from creditors.

- A credit score is a 3 digit number that is a product sold with your credit report. It is based upon your credit history and gives lenders an idea of how likely you are to repay your debt.

- You have <u>three</u> scores – one for each of the major credit bureaus. And those scores may not be the same. It's important to verify that they are similar, as disparities could mean that one or more of the bureaus have different information that may not be factual or is missing.
- There are five areas that impact scores. Those areas are:
  - o Payment history (which accounts for 35% of the score)
  - o Balances owed on accounts (which accounts for 30%)
  - o Length of credit history (which accounts for 15% of the score)
  - o New credit (which accounts for 10%)
  - o Mix of credit (which accounts for 10% of the score)
- The credit score is a snapshot of the time in which the credit report is pulled. It takes time for some items to be reported to the bureaus. And the credit report reflects the previous month's activity, not always the current month.
- The older the negative history, the less impact it has on your credit. Therefore, a 60 day late from several years back has less impact than a more current 30 day late within the past year.
- The magic number in credit is 7. For the most part, negative credit history only remains on our reports for seven years.

***

C hapter 3

A Second Set of Rules: The Fair Credit Reporting Act

The Fair Credit Reporting Act (FCRA) was designed to allow every consumer the rights to accuracy, fairness and privacy in their credit reports. The FCRA is the cornerstone of the laws and procedures consumer reporting agencies (credit bureaus) and creditors (lenders) must follow. The credit reports provided by the credit bureaus are supposed to contain correct and complete information. Considering the primary purpose of a credit report is to allow businesses (typically lenders or service providers) to make a decision, it is vital that the information be factual.

The truth about credit reports is that a large amount of inaccurate information exists. Congress passed the FCRA for the simple reason that consumers need a way to protect themselves. The existence of the Act gives consumers the ability to correct, update, amend and take action regarding the content of a credit report.

The Act only works if a consumer takes action. Unfortunately, many consumers are not aware of their rights. Furthermore, many consumers do not review their credit reports to discover incorrect information. While the credit bureaus are aware of the law, they are providing information given by creditors. Since the credit bureaus only report the information they receive, the burden of verification rests on the shoulders of consumers and creditors.

There are over 1 billion entries per month by the credit bureaus. The likelihood of error is great. Entry mistakes, computer malfunctions and other slip-ups create potential for any number of mistakes in credit reporting. Common ways mistakes occur:

- Applying under different names such as James Smith or James Smith-Oliver can lead to problems.
- Clerical errors occur inputting a loan application.
- Inaccurate social security numbers may be provided, or are input incorrectly by a lender.
- Information may be inadvertently applied to the wrong account.

And the list goes on...

There are seven basic rights in the FCRA that every consumer should know:

1. **You must be told if information in your file has been used against you.** If you apply for a loan and are not granted the loan, you must be informed if information from your credit report played a role in the denial. Not only do loan denials require this, but if you are denied services you must be notified.

   Sharon is ready to move into her new home and she calls the utility company. The utility company wants a history of payment from Sharon's previous utility provider. However, the utilities were in her former roommate's name. Now the utility company wants to *look at Sharon's credit report. They look for a score that meets their risk threshold of whether payments by Sharon can be expected to be made on time. Sharon's credit score does not meet the specified threshold and she is required to make a deposit of $200. The deposit acts as collateral for her to prove the payments will be made. Sharon will soon receive a letter acknowledging the decision was made based on information contained in her credit report. It will identify which of the credit bureaus provided the information.*

In the above example we don't necessarily know the threshold required to not have to make that deposit for service. The required score could be 700. If Sharon's score is under a 700, it doesn't mean her credit is bad. Sharon just needs to check her report to ensure there is nothing hurting her credit scores.

Make sure that you get a notice of denial in writing. The notice should detail which credit bureau was used when pulling your credit information. The importance of being notified when a denial takes place is that you are alerted that something negative could be on your credit report.

***

When you apply for a credit offer and do not receive the presented interest rate, this is often the result of not meeting the scoring criteria for the offer. The resulting new offer may not be an indication of something negative if the criteria of the original offer was to have 720 credit. When credit is denied completely, this is the time for concern. When a consumer is denied credit due to information contained in a credit report, a free copy of the report may be requested from the reporting bureau.

Anytime a consumer is made aware that a credit report showed information resulting in denial, it is imperative to get a copy of the credit report ASAP. The denial of credit is the initial tip-off that something could be wrong with the credit report.

It is important to become proactive in knowing the contents of our credit reports. A denial could also be the tip-off that we have been the victim of identity theft. The bottom line is that there are numerous possibilities of why we could be denied credit based on our credit report. An unknown late payment, a medical collection, a reporting error…the list is endless. However, identifying the reason as quickly as possible is the first step. Once identified the next step is to assess whether any negative information is erroneous. The steps to correct inaccurate information are addressed later in this book.

2. **You can find out what is in your file at any point in time.** Everyone in the country is now entitled to one free credit report annually. When you get a copy of your credit report it is important to make sure you get a copy from all three of the major credit bureaus. You may receive what is known as a "Tri-merge" credit report which is one report containing all three bureau reports. Otherwise, get each individual report. The three major credit bureaus are Experian, Equifax and TransUnion.

When you do get a copy of your credit report, it is a good idea to keep it with your important paperwork. There are some good reasons why you would want to do this:
   - If you ever encounter a problem with your credit, you have a record of how it once stood.

Perhaps something appears at a later point that is not yours. You can match up the two reports to look for any differences.

- Lost your wallet? What's the first thing you need to do? Contact the credit card companies immediately to let them know your credit may have been compromised. *(I lost my wallet once and because I saved all my statements I was able to call the credit card companies to report the loss. I was fortunate that the information was readily available to me. The following day I was contacted by one credit card company and told someone had tried to use my card. Due to my call, the account had been frozen and the card was unusable.)* For most of us, if we need to contact a credit card company we look at the back of the card. Sort of hard to do when the card is lost or stolen. Write that Customer Service number down on your credit report and then you have everything you need in one place, just in case. (In some cases, the phone number may already be printed on your credit report along with your account information. But you want to double-check to make sure).

- Track your progress as your credit improves. From an emotional standpoint it's reassuring to watch yourself progress as your balances are paid down.

- The credit report acts as an instant accounting of who and how much you owe.

When you do save a copy of your credit report, make sure it is in a secure place. A locked filing cabinet or a safe deposit box is best. You may want to take a black marker over your social security number and personal information. Marking over your account numbers is also a good idea. Leave the last four digits readable to separate cards from the same company. The lender should be able to identify your account based on your social security number, not just your account number.

***

The ability to find out what is contained in your credit report is one of the most important aspects of the FCRA. Probably equal to the ability to correct inaccurate information. When was the last time you looked at your credit report? When I pose this question to my clients the most common answer is: Never. And some statistics have shown that less than 20% of Americans have viewed their credit report. So my clients' answers are not shocking.

If you do one thing to better your finances this year, get a copy of your credit report. Review the information in it; do everything you can to understand it. Most people do not become aware of a credit problem until they apply for a loan. Unfortunately that is the wrong time to find out there is something negative on the credit report. Even if the negative item is incorrect, it can take 30 days or more to be removed and your credit rating restored. The end result of not knowing your personal credit is likely the denial of credit or paying more with higher interest rates.

3. **You can dispute inaccurate information with the credit bureaus or the creditor.** If you determine that

something is incorrect on your credit report, it's time to make a dispute. This is where the frustration with the credit system can begin for most consumers.

Disputing inaccurate information involves an entire section of this book. But here are the basics. When disputing with the credit bureaus, you will write a letter detailing your dispute. You will send a copy of that letter to **all three** credit bureaus. Sending the dispute to all bureaus is very important. On countless occasions I have pulled a credit report for a client only to see a previously corrected item appear on the other two credit bureaus' reports. Remember, banks typically use the middle of the three credit scores. If one report is correct but the other two are not, that middle score may be low.

Donnie finds out he was denied a loan due to information contained on an Experian report. Donnie determines the negative information is incorrect and corrects it with Experian. But Donnie forgets to check out his reports with Equifax and TransUnion. Donnie tries for a loan again and gets denied. This time the lender was using a credit report from TransUnion. Donnie checks that report and realizes that it contains the same erroneous information that was on the Experian report.

Donnie had a 580 score when the denial took place. The Experian score was 580, the Equifax was 585 and TransUnion had a score of 570. The middle score, the score most banks will use, was Experian's score of 580. After the correction, Donnie's Experian score goes up to 720. When Donnie applied again, the Equifax and TransUnion scores were still the same as before since nothing was corrected with those two bureaus. So at the time of the second loan application, Donnie's scores were 720, 585 and 570. That made his middle score

Equifax's 585. Doesn't sound so good, huh? Donnie is stuck pretty much where he began, with a score in the 500s. The difference between his scores is huge and a better middle score would greatly affect his interest rate.

All disputes must be done with all three credit bureaus. Once the dispute letter is written, it is ideal to send copies of any supporting documentation along with the letter. When sending copies of documentation it is a good idea to highlight the parts supporting your claim.

***

*Shannon has a bankruptcy discharged. Items from the bankruptcy still show on her credit report as being owed. The correct way for such accounts to appear is to state "Included in Bankruptcy" and show a zero balance. Often accounts included in a bankruptcy will not be updated to reflect the discharge of the debt. Shannon needs to send a copy of the discharge papers (discharge and all schedules) along with the letter to **each** of the three credit bureaus.*

What if you have no supporting documentation? Depending on what you are disputing you may be able to acquire documentation from the reporting creditor. In fact, it is a good idea to contact the offending creditor directly as soon as you become aware of the infraction. Many times an error by a creditor will be fixed once it is pointed out. Ultimately, what is on the credit report is all that matters, be diligent and keep pursuing the matter until your credit report is reflecting what is accurate.

Late payments can knock a credit score down dramatically. When I pull credit it is not uncommon to see a late payment that my client says could not possibly be true. I recommend contacting the creditor to see what they say. In some cases the creditor says that it was a mistake and that it will be fixed. Keep in mind that when a creditor changes what it is reporting on you, it can take 30 days before it goes on your report. Most creditors report once a month. If the creditor agrees it has made a reporting error, always request written documentation. You will still want to dispute with the credit bureaus and now you have documentation regarding the error. If a mistake can happen once, it can easily happen two or three more times. Put your documentation of the error in a safe place and plan on keeping it.

***

Be warned, disputing with the credit bureaus can be tedious and frustrating. Sometimes it does take longer than 30 days and results may vary. See **Chapter 7** for a more in depth look at disputing, and see the example letters in the back of the book.

4. **Incorrect information on the credit report must be corrected or deleted.** Once it is determined something is incorrect on your credit report, it must be addressed by the credit bureaus.

5. **You can dispute inaccurate items with the source of the information.** This would be a two-pronged approach in removing inaccurate information. It is always worth the time to dispute with both the credit bureaus and the source of the information. However, when disputing directly with the "source," you may

find differing results. You may find that when dealing with a credit card company you are likely to get better results than dealing with a collection agency.

A credit card company is an example of an original source, whereas a collection agency is most likely reporting "hand-me-down" information from the original source of the debt. If you see a late payment from a credit card company you can call its Customer Service Department to inquire about the information. The Customer Service Representative will have all the information pertaining to your account available to them. The Rep can tell you when your payment was received, when it was due, if you were over your limit and so on.

In contrast, at a collection agency you would be speaking with a person whose number one priority is to collect a debt. The collector will only know who the original creditor was, the amount owed and how long it has been owed. The only reason to call a collection agency directly is to settle a debt, find out how much is owed or who the original creditor was. In some cases, you may need to contact a collector to get a "paid" statement for your debt. Most likely you will not want to contact the collection agency directly to argue because it is unlikely to get the results you want. In contacting the original creditor you are not likely to get many answers either. Typically you will be told the account has been placed in collection and given the contact information for the collector.

Since it is so difficult to find out information about a collection in order to dispute it, be sure to do all you can to dispute a past due amount before it ever goes to collection. Granted, it may be easier to negotiate a lower payoff once it is with a collection agency.

However, your best shot of preventing a past due account from hurting your score the most is to take care of it before it gets sent to collection.

6. **Outdated information may not be reported.** For the most part, outdated information would be anything over seven years old. Although we covered the exceptions to this earlier. When it comes to outdated information, only that information pertaining to credit scores would fall into the category of removal. A late payment over seven years old would have an impact on the credit score and therefore would have to be removed. Whereas incorrect employment information would not have to be removed since it does not pertain to the credit scores. Neutral information such as employment can be addressed, but does not fall under the law.

Late payments, collections, charge-offs, past due accounts...anything that would reflect negatively on credit scores has a seven year life. But, as I pointed out in the previous chapter, there are different rules for bankruptcy, tax liens and judgments.

Jackie's account became delinquent in January 2005. The account went to collection in August 2005. The date of the collection will report as January 2005 on the credit report because this is when the account first became delinquent.

Over the next several years, Jackie's account is assigned to a succession of collection agencies. However, the reporting time limit is still based on the original date of delinquency from which the account was never brought current.

7. **Access to your file is limited to those you have given permission to.** The Fair Credit Reporting Act makes it

a federal crime to knowingly and willfully obtain a person's credit report without their consent or under false pretenses. It is a felony and punishable with a fine and up to two years in prison.

For the most part, potential creditors ask for your permission to review your credit report. Signing a credit application is typically considered written permission to view a credit report. Users of consumer reports must have a permissible purpose to obtain such information. To protect consumer privacy the use of consumer reports is limited. Permissible purpose would be:

- As ordered by a court or a federal grand jury subpoena.
- As instructed by the consumer in writing.
- For the extension of credit as a result of an application from a consumer, or the review of a consumer account.
- Employment purposes as long as the consumer has given written permission.
- The underwriting of insurance as a result of a consumer application.
- When there is a legitimate business need for a transaction initiated by the consumer.
- To review a consumer account to determine whether the consumer continues to meet the terms of the account.
- To determine eligibility of a consumer for a license or other benefit granted by a governmental entity required by law to consider an applicant's financial responsibility or status.
- For use by a potential investor or servicer, or current insurer, in a valuation or assessment of the credit or prepayment risk associated with an existing credit obligation.

- For use by state and local officials in connection with the determination of child support payments, or modifications and enforcement.

What about those "prescreened" offers?

Under the FCRA, creditors and insurers are permitted to gain limited information from consumer reports to make unsolicited offers. Direct marketers of such offers obtain a list of consumers from credit reporting agencies. The list of consumers will meet specified criteria, such as a geographic location or credit scores that fall in a certain range. The solicitor must provide a statement to the consumer making notice of:
- Information in a consumer file was used in connection with the transaction.
- The offer was received by the consumer because they met a criteria of credit worthiness used in screening for the offer.
- The offer may not be extended if after the consumer responds, it is determined the consumer does not meet the criteria used in screening.
- The consumer may opt-out of future offers generated by the information contained in his or her consumer file. The address and toll-free telephone number for opting-out must be provided.

Landlords and Credit Reports

Many landlords use credit reports when deciding whether or not to rent to a potential tenant. Instead of a full credit report sometimes a tenant screening service is used. Anytime a landlord uses information from a third party to make a decision the action is covered under the Fair Credit Reporting Act. This would not be the case if the landlord checked references on their own or had an employee make a verification.

If a landlord takes an adverse action against a rental applicant it is important to be within the law for such actions. An adverse action could be:

- Denying the application
- Requiring a co-signer for the lease
- Requiring a deposit or larger deposit that would not be required by another applicant
- Raising the rent to a higher amount than for another applicant

Any time an adverse action takes place based on information provided in a consumer report the landlord is required to provide a notice to the applicant. This must include:

- The name, address and telephone number of the agency that provided the information, including a toll-free number for nationwide agencies.
- A statement that the agency did not make the decision, although they did supply the information. The agency cannot give specific reasons for the adverse action.
- Notice of the applicants right to dispute inaccurate information provided by the reporting agency. The applicant also has a right to a free copy of the report from the agency if requested within 60 days of the notice.

Failing to provide notice could lead to legal consequences for a landlord. Individuals may sue in federal court and the FTC could sue for non-compliance of the Fair Credit Reporting Act.

Employment

Credit reports have become commonplace when screening job applicants. The typical background check includes a credit check for many potential employees.

A potential employer can find out how much you owe on your mortgage, your car and your credit cards as well as how often you've been late on your bills. Everything that a credit report would contain could be available to your potential employer. In the case of bankruptcy, an employer is not allowed to discriminate. This is not the same as protection from discriminatory treatment based on your financial history, however. It is just the right to deal with financial troubles through bankruptcy that is protected. Translation: An employer can't hire or fire you because you claimed bankruptcy. But an employer can choose to hire or fire you if your financial history shows you may not be responsible in the tasks required on the job. So, employers can use credit problems such as defaults or collections actions in their hiring decisions. They just have to take care when making such decisions.

Since your credit report can play a major role in getting a job, this illustrates the importance of checking the credit report for mistakes. Here is a good example of how an error can cost someone a job:

Jamie applies for a job and is informed that due to her credit report she will not be hired. She gets a copy of her credit report and discovers a student loan is erroneously reporting she was late for six months in a row. She knows it is a mistake because it was during the time she was in graduate school. The student loan company reported the late payments prior to when it became aware she was still in school and therefore her loans were in deferment. The late payments were not corrected and stayed on the credit report. When Jamie applied for her job, the employer saw the late payments and denied her employment based on what the credit report contained. She should remedy the mistake and attempt to reapply for the position. Situations like this occur and it illustrates the importance of a correct credit report not only for borrowing money, but also for gaining employment.

An employer is required to tell you if information in your credit file is used against you. If an employer uses credit information to deny an applicant a job, fire a current employee, rescind a job offer or cancel a promotion, federal law requires that employer to do two things:

1. Before the "adverse action" is actually taken, the employer is supposed to provide the worker with a copy of the report and an explanation of the worker's Fair Credit Reporting Act rights.
2. After the action is taken, the worker must be told which credit bureau provided the credit file information, given contact information and informed of the right to dispute the accuracy of the report.

*   Most of the laws that protect you the consumer in regards to accuracy, fairness and privacy are contained in the Fair Credit Reporting Act (FCRA).
*   You should check your reports regularly. The chance for error is significant. And this can result in erroneous negative information on your report.
*   If information in your credit report is used against you in a hiring decision, a lending decision, etc. then you must be informed.

- You have the right to look at your credit report file at any time. And when you do, it's wise to keep the copies in a safe place.
- You can dispute incorrect information with the credit bureaus. When you make a dispute, do so to all three bureaus. And send supporting documentation when you have it.
- When it is determined through investigation by the bureaus that there is indeed incorrect information in your file, that information must be corrected or deleted.
- You can also dispute inaccurate information with the source of the information – the original lender.
- The credit bureaus are not permitted to report outdated information.
- No one may have access to your file except those you have given permission to. However, there are those entities which may have a "permissible purpose" for accessing that information under certain circumstances.

***

Chapter 4

The Credit Report

"The only way around is through." - *Robert Frost*

Overview

The credit report is the data recorder of our personal credit history. It tracks our actions in regards to our credit. Credit reporting agencies collect information from "reporters," otherwise known as creditors, government entities, collection agencies, and third-party intermediaries. The information contained in the report is what generates credit scores. If something is wrong in regards to your credit, the report is where you will find it. This is also where you would begin fixing your credit.

How common is it for a credit report to be wrong? According to the U.S. Public Interest Research Group, up to 25% of credit reports contain errors serious enough to result in the denial of credit. Most reports will have a minor error of some sort. The numbers are staggering. According to the Congressional Research Service, each credit bureau has records on 1.5 billion accounts held by 210 million individuals. It would be difficult not to get some serious errors weaved into a number of reports. While most incorrect information contained in a credit report will not result in the denial of credit, even the minor items should be looked into. You never know what you might find.

Report Explanation

It seems like every credit report has some variation in how it is structured. There are hundreds of credit report providers across the country, which draw information from the three major credit bureaus to help lenders and service providers to render decisions. Since it is important to be able to understand what your credit report is conveying, I decided to identify the format of the free annual credit report:

Name of Creditor: The entity reporting the information

Address of Creditor: Mailing address for correspondence

Creditor Phone: Customer service contact (not always provided)

Account Number: The number that identifies the account as yours

Status: Will show one or more of the following: *Paid, Closed, Open, Current, Past Due, Number of days late, Never Late, Inactive*

Date Opened: The original date the account was opened

Type: Installment, revolving, mortgage, auto, etc.

Credit Limit: In the case of a revolving account this shows the total available limit for the account

Original Amount: In the case of an installment loan this shows what the starting balance was

Reported Since: This will usually correlate with the *"Date Opened,"* however, this can sometimes vary if the account was not immediately reported or if there was a change in the account number

Terms:	For an installment loan the number of months the loan will last is listed; for a revolving account it may list *N/A*
High Balance:	For a revolving account it lists the highest amount the account balance has ever reached; for an installment loan it will typically show *N/A* or the original amount of the loan
Date of Status:	This will typically correlate with the last date reported or will show the last date of account activity
Monthly Payment:	For a revolving account this shows the minimum payment due; for an installment loan this shows the agreed upon monthly payment
Recent Balance:	Current amount owed on the account
Last Reported:	Last date reported by the creditor, an account could be reported on even when there is no recent activity, this would be common for a revolving account
Responsibility:	Individual or joint (co-signed)
Recent Payment:	The amount of the last payment received
Account History:	Displays the number of days late and the dates the late payments occurred
Balance History:	Shows the monthly balance for the past two years

On the free annual credit report it will list accounts with negative items first and all positive accounts after that. The last few digits of each account will not be displayed.

After the account section it will list all inquiries made on your credit report for the past two years. The next section lists all personal information including:

- Name variations
- Date of birth
- Addresses - both current and previous dating almost ten years
- Spouse's first name
- Employers (although sometimes this information will be missing)
- Your telephone numbers

The rest of the report gives your consumer rights under the Fair Credit Reporting Act including information on disputing. It is possible to dispute online for free with the free annual credit report, which is very helpful. If you dispute through the online offering of the annual credit report the investigation can take up to 45 days.

Credit Reports

Credit reports can differ in structure depending on the source. The most important core information you need to review:

- Verify the information on your identity. Make sure the report has your correct name, birth date, address, and social security number. Many times your employment information will be incorrect. You may want to try calling the credit bureaus to update your employment information if this concerns you. Employment does not influence your credit score. However, if it does not match the employment you put on a loan application this could raise a red flag with an underwriter.
- Be sure you recognize the debts appearing on your report. Unfamiliar accounts should be looked into for accuracy. Keep in mind that some accounts could be reported by a parent company. In the case of department store cards, it could report with a different

name than the actual department store you applied through.

- Check the payment history for any late payments. If you have late payments on a revolving account it is worth calling to inquire about them. If you have an account with one late payment and it is open you should contact the credit card to see if they will remove the late based on your otherwise unblemished record. Some credit cards will do this, others will not. If you have closed the account there is almost zero chance they will remove anything since you are no longer their customer.

- Check your current balances and available limits on revolving accounts. Remember you want to always try to keep your balances under 50% of the available limit. Check to make sure your revolving accounts are reporting a limit. Some cards do not report a limit and then the ratio is based on whatever your highest balance reached. If you have never taken your balance very high you may want to pick a month to take it as high as you can so that you do not have to worry about your ratio down the road. Do not do this if you are a couple months away from a major purchase as this will take two to three months to be beneficial. You would not want to get caught with a really high balance at the time you are applying for new credit.

- Make sure any previously disputed accounts are correct. There are times when a successfully disputed account is changed back to the incorrect way it was reporting originally. If it was a computer glitch or someone with your same name there is always the possibility it will come up as an issue again in the future.

- Look for the accounts that should be on the report. If you have accounts that are not reporting you will want to contact the creditor to find out the reason it has not been reported. In the case of new accounts it can take a few months before they show up on your credit report. Be patient.

Reason Codes

Reason codes are an indication of why the credit score is not higher. They can help people with low credit scores find ways to make improvements. For those people with high credit scores the reason codes may indicate something that would only make a slightly marginal increase.

Common reason codes found on credit reports:
- Amount owed on accounts is too high
- Too many accounts with balances
- Account payment history is too new to rate
- Too many inquiries in the last 12 months
- Too many accounts recently opened
- Number of accounts with delinquency
- Serious delinquency
- Derogatory public record or collection filed

The problem with these "reason codes" is that they don't always tell the whole story. People with good scores may see "Too many accounts with balances" and have only one account with a $10 balance. The reason codes are basically telling you why your credit score is not perfect. Someone with an 800 score should not be concerned with what the reason codes are indicating. A person with lower credit should use the reason codes as a way to identify what is having the worst effect on their credit scores. In some cases they may be able to take action, but sometimes the only thing that will help is the passing of time as a negative item ages.

2 Account History vs. 10 Account History

There are numerous variables when it comes to credit, but when it comes to the amount of history a credit report contains this is not an even playing field. A consumer with two accounts has a thin credit file. It is recommended to have at least 3 open and active (within the past 6 months) accounts that have been open for at least three years. Is this imperative? Not necessarily. It depends on what the consumer needs down the road. Does it make it easier to borrow money later? Yes, especially when purchasing a property using niche mortgage programs such as stated income, no documentation, zero down interest only, etc.

The person with only a 2 account history is at a serious disadvantage if something negative were to happen to their report. One 30 day late payment might knock the score down 50 points. Depending on how long the two existing accounts have been open, the damage from a late payment may be more or less severe. If the accounts were less than a year old the overall picture would be worse than if both accounts were over five years old or more. People with thin credit files need to pay extra attention to how they manage their payments and debts because there is little room for error. One slip-up could all of a sudden make them a subprime borrower in some circumstances.

The consumer who has 10 accounts open and active is in a position I would compare to a diversified stock portfolio. If something were to happen to one of the accounts you have such a mix that the others will keep the scores from going down too far. If you have ten stocks and one goes down, the other nine hopefully are good enough to keep the overall picture in good standing.

Brenda and Dawn are best friends. Both have accounts over 5 years old and have always paid their bills on time. And both have a score of 720. They take a long vacation in

Maui and both forget to make a payment on their bills. So Brenda and Dawn both receive a 30 day late on their credit reports. Both women order their credit scores to see how much of a hit they took. Brenda's score after the 30 day late shows a respectable 690. Yet Dawn's score dropped further, to 630. Why the difference? Brenda has 8 accounts and Dawn has only 2 open and active accounts. So Brenda has more positive credit history to cushion the impact of the negative information. Dawn has less history and therefore takes a bigger drop to her score.

Multiple open accounts provide a greater layer of protection. It can also heal the wounds of a negative occurrence quicker.

Credit scores are garbage in garbage out; you have to have positive stuff going in for a positive score to come out. When something bad does happen we need the positive to keep pouring in to offset the thing that is lowering the scores.

***

There is nothing wrong with only having two open and active accounts. As long as nothing negative occurs. A late payment or a collection can really send the scores out of whack compared to the counterpart with ten open active accounts. Unfortunately these things happen when we least expect them and sometimes without our knowledge.

Credit Report Examination

To get a good understanding of how credit reports and credit scores correlate we need to look at some real examples of credit histories.

Tammy has a middle score of 811. This is a very good score. Most likely Tammy's report has a long positive history. In reality, Tammy's credit report only contains one account. It is a revolving credit card and does not belong to Tammy; it is an authorized user account. The credit card account belongs to Tammy's mother. Tammy was added by her mother to the account strictly as authorized to use the card. The account was opened in 1990 and is still open today. There are no late payments showing up and the current balance is 1% of the available limit. This demonstrates the power credit cards can have as far as boosting scores and how we can share our history with authorized users. Being added as an authorized user on a positive credit card account with a lengthy history is one of the quickest ways to boost an established credit score, or to generate a score.

George has a score of 596, not a good score. At a 596 we might expect that George made some late payments at some point, and perhaps had a collection. None of that is the case with George's report. Not a single late payment or collection. However, there are six credit cards that are either over the limit or are right at the limit. The credit cards average out at five years old, so length of time established is not an issue. In fact, George has accounts dating back to the mid 1990's that are still open and active. The reason that George's scores are low is because being above or at the limit on credit cards is a bad thing for the credit scores. Yet George's situation isn't so bad. George merely has to pay down the balances to rebound the scores.

Catherine has a score of 697, a respectable score. Her report is full of well established revolving credit card accounts at zero balance. The reason Catherine's scores are not higher is because she made 2 late mortgage payments in the past 24 months, and 1 in the past 12 months. One of her credit cards has a late payment in the past 12 months. Typically, these negative items would knock the average credit score down into the 500's. But Catherine's report is so full of positive information that despite the severity and recent timeframe of the negative items, her scores are still good at 697. This is perfect evidence of why we need to build our positive credit up for a rainy day. Even people with great credit have a bad day sometimes. Without the negative items Catherine's credit scores would probably be in the high 700's or low 800's.

Lastly we take a look at Louise, who has a score of 530. This is a low score. The highlight of her report is that there was a bankruptcy three years ago and foreclosure two years before that. Half of Louise's accounts in the bankruptcy have been updated to show zero balance and zero past due. The other half still shows as being owed or still past due. There are several collections after the bankruptcy took place. On the positive side Louise has three open and active accounts. However, one of her accounts has been late twice in the past six months. Louise's report will take some time to rebound. Louise needs to be on-time with her payments and must stop allowing things to go to collection. The worst thing someone can do after a bankruptcy is to be late, or to let debts go to collection.

Free Credit Reports

Upon your request, the three major credit bureaus will provide you with a copy of your credit report. You are entitled to a free credit report every 12 months. The credit report you are entitled to does not include your credit scores. Remember, credit scores are not a part of the credit report, but rather a product sold with a credit report. In all likelihood this is the one piece of information that the majority of consumers are hoping to see. Consumers are able to purchase their credit scores when they get their free credit reports.

It is possible to dispute items online with the credit bureaus when you receive your free credit report through the internet. You are given a drop down menu to select the nature of the inaccurate item and you are able to type a brief explanation about the item.

There is only one official website to access your free credit report: www.annualcreditreport.com. You can get your credit report by telephone by calling 1-877-322-8228. To make a request by mail you can go to www.ftc.gov to print the Annual Credit Report Request Form. The mailing address is on the form. You will need to provide your name, address, social security number, and date of birth. In some situations a security question may be asked that only you would be able to answer. If you request your report on the website it will be available immediately. Making the request by telephone or mail will take approximately 15 days. It is possible that further information will be required to verify your identity and this could cause a delay.

***

The Annual Credit Report became law under the Fair and Accurate Credit Transactions Act (FACT Act), which is an amendment to the Fair Credit Reporting Act. The website www.annualcreditreport.com is maintained by the three nationwide credit bureaus, Equifax, Experian, and TransUnion.

Beware of imposter websites. Other websites offering free credit reports are not part of the legally mandated free credit report through Annual Credit Report. The imposter sites are typically looking to accomplish two things:

1. Lure you into signing up for credit monitoring services. You will be offered a free trial period of monitoring, which after the free trial period could result in an annual or monthly fee showing up on your credit card. If you are asked for a credit card number it is not a free offer. For those people who are interested in credit monitoring a good strategy is to only request your free report from one credit bureau at a time. If you request your free report from only one bureau every 3 to 4 months you achieve a more frequent monitoring than requesting all three reports every 12 months.

2. Collect your personal information to use in identity theft. Identity theft is thriving and criminals masquerading as an official website for The Annual Credit Report make it easy to get all your information in one spot.

Keep in mind that you will never receive solicitations from the Annual Credit Report folks. According to both the FTC and Annual Credit Report, if you receive an email, telephone call or any other solicitation whether by mail or internet pop-up it is an imposter. You should never provide your information to anyone making a free credit report solicitation.

The FTC has handed down a hefty fine of $950,000 to entities that have participated in tricking consumers into signing up for services under the guise of the Annual Credit Report. Letters from the FTC have warned 130 imposter sites that any attempt to mislead consumers is illegal. When you do type in www.annualcreditreport.com double check to make sure you have spelled it correctly. There are many sites that have various misspellings of the official site hoping to land visitors/victims that way. Also be careful when searching through a search engine, make sure you are in the correct site.

There are ways to get a free credit report outside of the Annual Credit Report guidelines of every 12 months. The following circumstances would allow someone to request a free credit report directly from the credit bureaus:

- Denied credit, insurance, or employment based on information contained in a credit report. You must make the request within 60 days of the denial notice. The free report may be obtained from the credit bureau(s) that provided the report upon which the decision was based. In some cases you may find that only one bureau was used, while in some cases it was all three of the credit bureaus.
- For those who are unemployed and are seeking employment within 60 days a free report will be provided (one in a 12 month period). A welfare recipient is entitled to a report every 12 months as well.
- If the credit report has been compromised due to fraud or identity theft a free credit report will be provided. Or if your credit report has been revised based upon an investigation into inaccurate information (in such a case you should automatically receive a copy from each bureau you disputed with at the conclusion of the investigation).

The purpose of looking at your credit report is to verify the information is correct. A large percentage of people have never looked at their credit reports. The system of allowing everyone a free credit report every 12 months was put in place to encourage people to be proactive in maintaining the accuracy of the information contained in credit reports. It is up to the consumer to catch mistakes and take action to fix inaccurate information.

It isn't just the three national credit bureaus that we are most familiar with that are required to provide us with a free report of our consumer file. ChoicePoint is a parent company that provides information on consumers through three of its separate companies.

- C.L.U.E. Inc. maintains information on insurance claims
- ChoicePoint WorkPlace Solutions Inc. maintains employment history information
- Resident Data Inc. maintains tenant history information

These companies are all subject to the free disclosure requirement under FACTA. ChoicePoint notes that not everyone will have a consumer report contained by these companies. If you have not had an insurance claim in the past five years you will not appear in the C.L.U.E. database. Likewise, if you have not been associated with clients of WorkPlace Solutions Inc. or Resident Data Inc., there will be no record of you in the system. If you would like to get more information, check out www.choicepoint.com.

***

Companies like ChoicePoint provide specialty consumer reports and are not under the same requirements as the three major credit bureaus. There is no centralized source for obtaining specialty reports. The only rule is that they establish a toll-free number for requests. Many of the national specialty reporting agencies have posted information on their websites, although this is not required under the new law.

According to the FTC, if you have problems with the Annual Credit Report system they need to hear from you. It's still a new system and it is hard to make changes unless consumers make issues known. Since the FTC shoulders the enforcement of credit regulations, it is important to make issues known. Don't assume someone else will do it.

Specialty Reports

The C.L.U.E. report is generated by one of the two major property claim databases, Comprehensive Loss Underwriting Exchange and Automated Property Loss Underwriting System. The property claim databases allow insurers to check the claim history on either an individual or a property. This is a benefit to consumers as they are able to get a C.L.U.E. report on the home they are planning to buy. The C.L.U.E. report is becoming well known in the real estate industry as many buyers are requesting them when they make an offer on a property. By requesting the C.L.U.E. report when the offer to buy is made the buyer will be alerted to any previous claims made on the property. Claims on a property can make a difference in what the policy amount will be. It can also act as an indicator. I had a client who backed out of a transaction when it was discovered a claim had been made from a burglary a few months prior to the home going on the market.

ChexSystems is a database service provided to banks that tracks negative information in regards to checking and savings accounts. This would typically be in the form of bounced checks, or non-sufficient funds. ChexSystems also verifies whether someone has provided a false social security number.

A negative ChexSystems report stays on record for five years and could prevent a consumer from opening a checking account. Nearly 80% of our nation's banks and credit unions belong to the ChexSystems network. ChexSystems estimates it saves the banking industry perhaps hundreds of million dollars from potential fraud.

- Your credit report is an accounting of your credit history. It's up to you to ensure the data on your credit report is correct.
- You will find "reason codes" on your report that give you an idea of why your score is not higher and what you need to do in order to improve your score. These reason codes may state things such as "serious delinquency" or "too many inquiries in past 12 months" and so on. Unfortunately, these reason codes are only short phrases that don't tell the whole story.
- It is recommended you have at least 3 open and active accounts. Believe it or not, when comparing people with 2 accounts versus 10 accounts, those with the 10 accounts are in a much better position. When something negative such as a late payment occurs, those with more accounts see less impact on their overall score. People with fewer accounts don't have much history to buffer those negatives and therefore receive a larger hit to their score.
- Take advantage of your free annual credit report! Online there is only one official website: www.annualcreditreport.com – make sure you don't get lured onto imposter sites! You can also call 1-877-322-8228 to request your free credit report.
- You also have the ability to access your credit report for free (outside of that annual free report) when you are denied credit or insurance, if you are unemployed for a period of time, etc. If you are the victim of identity

theft, you are worthy of free reports. Contact your credit bureaus and take advantage of these situations so you can stay on top of your credit information!

- There are also specialty reports that we have access to, such as the C.L.U.E. report that allows consumers to check the claims history on a property.

***

C hapter 5

Protecting and Improving Your Credit

"You must have long term goals to keep you from being frustrated by short term failures." - *Charles C. Noble*

There is a long running joke dating back to 30 years ago about the credit card bill for $0.00 that a person received in the mail. The card holder laughs at the notion of owing $0.00 and receiving a bill requesting $0.00. They throw away the bill only to receive a stern request for payment of $0.00 the next month. The next letter warns that $0.00 is now past due and that a default of $0.00 will ruin the credit if payment is not received. Finally the card holder sends a check for $0.00 and the ordeal ends. Silly? You bet! Frustrating? Sure! But it points out that we need to take every step and precaution possible to keep our scores from becoming damaged. Even if it means writing a check for $0.00.

Rapid Rescoring
Suppose there are errors on your credit report that are causing your credit scores to be lower than they should. Are you stuck with waiting for the entire process to take place before you can enjoy the benefits of higher credit scores? Not if you are applying for a mortgage; rapid rescoring can increase your credit scores in 48 to 72 hours.

This is a service offered by the credit agencies that sell credit reports (where mortgage companies get credit reports from) from the three major credit bureaus. The borrower provides documentation of what they are disputing and the credit agency goes directly to the credit bureaus to get it resolved. In doing this, if there is indeed a change on the credit report the scores will change immediately. The whole process happens generally in less than 72 hours depending on how busy the bureaus are at the time. I have had two bureaus turn a new score around in 24 hours and the third take 72 hours or vice versa.

There is no guarantee as to what the resulting credit score will be. However, I have seen scores go up as much as 70 points from rapid rescoring.

What is the catch? It costs money to do this. The average cost is $30 per bureau, per account, so at least $90 to make a change to one account with all three credit bureaus. It is not going to be the solution to every situation, but it is a handy tool when there is a glaring error. If it is apparent that a change in the scores is likely, then paying to put the credit report in the best light can be a wise move. If it will save someone money each month in financing it won't take long to make back the cost of the money spent for the rescore.

Opting Out

How many times have you received an offer in the mail telling you that you have been pre-approved for a credit card? These offers stem from your information being sold to marketers who solicit consumers. When you receive a "pre-approved" offer by mail be aware that it is a solicitation based on demographics you may have met on a direct marketing mailing list. They do not know enough about you or your credit to approve you without a full application.

How did you get on a mailing list?

- If you have a subscription to a magazine, belong to a club or association, made a donation to a charity or are a customer of a business this information is often available to direct marketers for a fee.
- List compilers comb public records to assemble databases for specific marketing campaigns.
- Under legally specified conditions credit reporting agencies offer pre-screened lists for companies to offer credit. This is the largest source of pre-approved offers you will receive. Reduction of pre-approved credit offers is a good way to protect you from identity theft. If the pre-approved offer goes to your previous mailing address you do not know whose hands it may fall into.

A 1996 amendment to the Fair Credit Reporting Act required that the credit bureaus provide an opt-out opportunity for consumers who do not want their names and addresses sold to credit grantors for solicitations. Consumers can and should take advantage of the right. To opt-out call: (888) 5OPTOUT, which is (888) 567-8688. You can go onto the FTC website for further information about opting out at www.ftc.gov. By opting out you will no longer receive pre-approved credit offers.

Now the latest deviation of the pre-screened offer is the "inquiry lead." When you apply for credit, within 24 hours several other banks may be notified of your application. You will start receiving telephone calls and mailers offering you lending products based on what you applied for. This is most common regarding mortgages. The problem is that many of these offers result bait-and-switch tactics. The telemarketer will make any promise they think a consumer wants to hear to try to lure the prospect away from the original lender. Here are some of the tactics being used:

- Saying they were notified by the original lender of the application and asked to call the consumer.
- Making specific promises that aren't met at closing.
- Sending out paperwork to consumers in hopes they will "accidentally" fill out and return the information, thus starting a file with the other lender.
- Hounding consumers about whether they are getting the best deal from their current lender.

This information does not come cheap, purchasing 50 leads will cost over $3,000. The standard conversion rate is 2%, so on 50 leads a lender can expect to get one closed loan. One closed loan at a cost of $3,000….. guess who is paying the price in their closing costs? If a telemarketing firm wishes to close 20 loans they would need to buy 1,000 leads at a cost of over $60,000. Do you think there might be a motive to say anything to get a consumer to go with their company? In the bait-and-switch game participants misconstrue information to make their offer look better. One example is to give a rate they call a 30-year rate, but it may actually be a 2-year adjustable rate amortized for 30 years. If a consumer leaves their recommended lender based on a slightly lower rate they may find out at the signing table they are actually getting a short-term rate instead of the 30-year fixed rate they wanted

Not only are telemarketers competing with the original lender, but they are competing amongst themselves. There are several companies buying this information from the credit bureaus and reselling it to telemarketers. Sellers of the 'inquiry data' market it as "like having a crystal ball telling you when someone fits your desirable lending profile". They do say conversion depends on the telemarketer's skill on the phone and ability to demonstrate a better offer. If you get a strange or unexpected call after applying for a loan, just hang up.

Can opting-out save the environment? Environmental advocates commonly use the statistic that each household receives enough junk mail to equal 1.5 trees. Although I did some research and came up with numbers that show 62,000,000 to 100,000,000 trees are used for junk mail each year. If you divide those numbers by the 213,000,000 people who have credit files and assuming the average household has two adults receiving junk mail, we are talking less than one tree per household. Opting-out will reduce offers of credit, and perhaps save a few saplings in the forest.

***

Automated Payments

Be careful when making automatic payments each month. There are plenty of stories out there that make you realize how dangerous it can be relying on them. Here is a situation involving a past client:

Annette has several real estate properties that are set up with automatic payments to be made each month. One particular month, Annette received calls from the lender on her voicemail but thought nothing of it. Instead of listening to what she thought was a sales pitch, Annette deleted the messages. Unfortunately, those calls were in reference to late payments on her properties. Annette had never had a problem with her automatic payments before, so she didn't think anything was wrong. She ended up with a 30 day late payment on two separate mortgages in the same month. The bank that had set up the automatic payments admitted in a letter that it was their fault, not Annette's. However, the companies collecting payment refused to remove the late payments. The lender did not have to reverse the late payments, because in actuality the payments were late. Annette persisted in her request to get the late payments removed. Her persistence paid off. The late payments were removed.

In a situation such as this never take "no" for an answer. Stay calm, keep the language clean, and keep going up the chain of command until you can get it resolved.

Since I have coached Annette on credit for years, her scores only dropped to about 690 with two mortgage lates in the same month. Normally Annette's score is in the high 700's, close to 800. Once the lates were removed we saw the scores return to the normal range.

Unfortunately, we only found out about the late payments showing on the credit report because we were financing a new purchase. Annette's scores were still in good range. However, most mortgage programs have strict guidelines regarding late mortgage payments within the past 12 to 24 months. Since it took much arm twisting to get the lender to confirm the late payments were not Annette's fault, we ended up having to go with a higher interest rate loan in the short term to close within the escrow timeframe.

This is a good example of how even people with pristine credit can get caught up in a tangled web of mistakes. Always watch the automated payments, be sure they have gone through. Ultimately it is the customer who has to ensure the payments have been made on time whether they are using a third party service or not. Remember this example the next time your bank calls, it could be for something other than a pitch to open another credit card.

Prior to applying for new credit make sure you have paid down your credit card balances to reduce the balance-to-owed ratio. Let's say you just took a vacation and put everything on your credit which you plan on paying off in full as soon as the bill arrives. It could take 30 to 60 days before your payment is reported on your credit report. If you were to apply for new credit prior to the payment being reported your credit scores may not be at their best. Think about it this way: If you make a payment in January it probably won't show up on your credit report until February or March.

***

Every credit card you have currently should be kept open forever. Be sure that you do use the credit cards you have at least a couple times throughout the year. The last thing you want is for your account to be closed due to inactivity. This can happen if a credit company determines your account is not making them any money by remaining stagnant. A good number of credit cards to have open and active is three. If you have more than three, don't worry about closing any accounts. Personally, I maintain ten that have been open for many years. Having more is a good thing as far as padding your overall length of credit history. If you have fewer than three it would be a good idea to acquire a couple over time. Just remember to never apply for a lot of credit in a short period of time as this is typically a red flag that there could be an issue coming in the near future (layoff, job loss, higher expenses, etc.) and it could knock your credit score down in the short term.

***

Store Financing

Avoid using in-store financing when making large purchases. We have all heard of "Buy now and pay nothing until next year," or even longer. The way this works is that you are being financed, but there are no payments due until the promotional period ends. Since these promotional periods can range from 90 days (same as cash) to three years, you are going to have an account with a finance company for at least that period of time. The way it shows up on a credit report is typically as a revolving account. If you make a purchase of $2,000 you will have an available limit of $2,000 and a balance of $2,000. Now you have a brand new account that is completely maxed out. This will certainly knock the credit scores down. A lot of people take the approach that they will just pay it off in full when the loan becomes due. Looking at the big picture, is it worth knocking your credit score down for 90 days to up to three years just to "Buy later?" During that period of time how much more will it cost you in interest to buy a car or a house? Depending on your overall credit picture it could be a tiny difference or it could be a major impact. In general a finance company loan on your credit report is not a healthy member of your credit. Finance companies can have a negative impact on the judgment of your credit from the fact that they generally lend at higher rates to riskier borrowers. In protecting our credit scores, every little bit helps. So avoid these types of loans if at all possible.

Store Credit Cards

You are standing at the cash register grimacing at the amount you are about to spend to make your purchase, then comes the infamous question, "Would you like to save 10% today on your purchase?" Of course we want to save money on our purchases, but what is the true cost of those short term savings? Let's say you are making a purchase of $300 and you agree to apply for the store credit card so that you can save 10% on your purchase. You save $30, but you could have just dropped your credit scores considerably. Typically the available limit on a store credit card is relatively low compared to that of a major credit card. If your purchase amount is $300, maybe you receive a credit limit of $500. Right off the bat the balance exceeds 50% of the available limit. Or it could be worse if the limit was placed right at your purchase amount of $300; now it's maxed out. Keep in mind the other factors in play with this situation: a new inquiry on the credit report and a new account. Adding all of these things up will generally result in a decline in the credit scores in the short term. The $30 savings at the register is a moot point if the result is a higher interest rate on a car or house. Be careful at the cash register, your purchases could end up costing you more than you'd ever think!

Medical Collections

A fair amount of collections result from a lack of communication. The most common collection is certainly medically related. Keep in mind that legally, the patient is responsible for their own bill, not an insurance company. If I go to the hospital it is <u>my</u> responsibility to make sure my insurance company pays what they are supposed to pay. Often times the health insurance company takes its time processing a claim to make sure that the claim is payable. The process may take a week or it may take months. Hospitals, doctors, dentists, etc. turn the bills over to a billing company, and after a certain point if the bill goes unpaid it finds its way to a collection agency. Many people assume that the insurance company will take care of it eventually and ignore the bills coming from the medical practice. Since most collections on credit reports are medical, ignoring the billing department is the wrong thing to do. We need to keep up the communication with the billing departments of the medical practices. Unfortunately insurance does not always cover everything. The worst way to find that out is to have it go to collection. Even worse is that you probably will not know it was sent to collection until you are ready to buy a home or a vehicle. Then the lender will ask about that pesky medical collection on your credit report.

Our objective is to prevent anything from ever going to collection in the first place. If there is uncertainty with an insurance claim it is important to keep the communication flowing between you and the billing department. Ask questions such as:

- When did you speak to the insurance company last?

- When do you expect to see payment from the insurance company?

- Do you have my correct insurance? *If you have switched jobs or your health provider has changed recently, it is quite possible the claim is being sent to the wrong insurance company. Confirm your correct information is on file with your medical provider.*

- Does my insurance company have the correct information on my coverage? *Call your insurance provider to confirm your information is correct. I had an issue with my son where the claim kept getting denied for his immunization shots. The problem was that we had recently switched insurance carriers and the new insurance provider had marked on my paperwork that there was "other" coverage for my son. This was not the case, it was fixed and the claim was paid. Do not assume things will just work out. You can avoid a lot of headaches at inopportune times by doing your own follow-up when a claim is not being paid.*

- At what point would this go to collection if the insurance does not pay the claim? *Some billing departments might go until the claim is officially denied. Others may only go three months and then demand payment whether from insurance or the patient.*

A point of confusion is when a medical visit results in three different bills. You may receive a bill from the hospital, the doctor, and a lab. Do not assume you have already paid for the medical visit if lingering bills show up. When my son was born I was sending out checks to everyone for everything. I even received a bill from a nurse for $16 and some change. It totally took me by surprise, but I sent the payment. I would rather be out $16 on something I may have been able to argue than to have my credit score drop because the $16 went to collection. A majority of the medical collections I see on credit reports are for less than $100. I cannot list the number of times people have asked, "Is this $100 medical collection going to increase my interest rate?" The answer might be "Yes." Be diligent about putting potentially bad situations to rest when the opportunity to do so is available.

Another bad situation is when you are the victim in a car accident. Let's say someone blew through a stop light and t-boned your car in the intersection. The ride in an ambulance to the hospital alone is probably going to cost a good amount of money. Who is going to pay the medical bills? If the other driver is cited then hopefully they have insurance to cover the bills. What do insurance companies like to do when they have a claim? Drag their feet and negotiate a lower cost. Since you were the patient, you are still responsible for the treatment incurred. This is a situation where you need to be extra cautious because your good name is on the line. Do not assume that an insurance company will just take care of everything. Make sure they do. Get on the telephone with the billing department of the hospital and make sure they are aware of the situation. Communicate, communicate, communicate, and make sure the lines of communication are going both ways. You do not want this situation to escalate into a collection. Talk about a slap in the face! An unfortunate and sad situation resulting in your financial downfall. But it happens all the time. We cannot make assumptions when it comes to people or companies paying out money. Especially when we have the most to lose under the circumstances.

Are medical collections more likely to occur depending on which health insurance carrier we have? The short answer is yes. When a hospital budgets for the year it expects to have a large percentage of its income written off to contractuals. Contractuals are payment arrangements made with HMO's, PPO's, Medicare, and Medicaid, etc. and other payers of health care costs. Essentially, different payers pay different amounts for identical services. In terms of health insurance, the contractual allowances will vary from company to company.

Perhaps insurance company A gets a 50% knockdown in cost and insurance company B gets a 20% knockdown in cost for the identical services. This will be based on how much business the companies do with the hospital. How does this affect medical collections? If company A is billed for $100 it will only owe $50, when company B is billed for $100 it will owe $80. Now let's say the patient was supposed to pay $20 of their own money. If I am the hospital I am going after the patient with insurance from company A first, because I received the least amount of payment from company A. In fact, I may even be willing to negotiate with the patient who has coverage with company B to pay less than $20 if they do not have the money. It all comes down to dollars, the insurance company that pays the least for identical services has customers who will go to collection quicker to recover the patient portion of the bill.

The Federal Reserve has concern about the appropriateness of medical collections in credit evaluations for several reasons:
- More likely to be in dispute
- Inconsistently reported
- May be of questionable value in predicting future payment performance
- Raises the issue of rights to privacy and fair treatment of the disabled or ill. (FACTA no longer allows the original medical source to be reported to the credit report)

***

Other Collections

If medical collections are the top collection problem on credit reports, cable television has to be a close second. The problem with cable billing is that it is not just about paying the cable bill itself. There can be problems with the return of equipment.

You are moving and the cable guy comes out to turn off the cable and take back the cable box. He gets back to the cable company, turns everything in, but whoops, forgets to credit you for your cable box. Years later you check your credit report and spot a hefty collection account from your local cable company.

I see a lot of $400 cable collections, which is the "cost" of a digital cable box in my area. People are always shocked to hear they have a collection from the local cable company when they know for a fact the final bill was paid. They call the cable company ready to rumble. The operator says, "It looks like you didn't turn in your digital cable box when your service was discontinued." The client swears up and down that it was turned in and no longer in their possession. The operator kindly asks, "Do you have a receipt showing you turned in the box?" The client says it must be somewhere, but they rarely find it.

When you move be sure to turn in the cable equipment on your own and get a receipt. Put the receipt in a safe place. A place safe enough for $400 because that's what the receipt is worth if a problem crops up. Anytime you get a receipt for returning equipment, whether it is for cable or something else, always save the receipt. If you pay a collection, a judgment, anything - always save the receipt or statement. These things have a way of coming back and trying to bite you and you'll need your evidence of payment.

Collections tend to bounce from collection agency to collection agency. Always try to pay by check and be sure to request the cancelled check from your bank when it has been paid. Some collection agencies will offer you a better deal if you pay immediately by credit card over the phone. Be sure to verify who you are talking to over the phone before ever giving out a credit card number. My advice is to call the original creditor (for example, the cable company) and ask who is currently collecting the money. Make sure it is the same company that called you. Then look up the number to the collection agency on your own and call back about your account. If you discovered the collection on your credit report there could be a contact number towards the back of your credit report. It would be listed under "Directory Information" or "Decode Directory Information." Be warned, some collection agencies have various names within the same company. It can get confusing when ABC Collections is also CBA Collections, which also is known as XYZ Collections.

***

Another source of collection misery? Security alarm companies. We all get the advertisements about receiving a free security system. The hitch is that you have to sign up for service on a lease ranging from 1 year to 3 years or more. Of course you can save some money each month by getting the longer term. Nobody can predict the future; you might move within a year for any number of reasons. If you sign a 3 year service contract and move after 1 year you still have to pay for the remaining 2 years. Only sign a 1 year agreement and if at all possible use a service provider that allows you to go month-to-month instead of long term. Saving a little more per month goes out the window if you need to sell your house before the term is up. I've seen countless people forced to payoff a year or more of security monitoring because of unforeseen circumstances. If it goes unpaid, you guessed it, it will likely show up as a collection on the credit report.

Timeshares

The unexpected foreclosure is when someone goes into default on a timeshare. I see these accounts all the time. Someone goes on vacation, gets pitched for a timeshare, signs up and then realizes it just isn't in the budget. When the creditor reports it, the account looks like real estate in your credit file. If someone becomes late it looks like they have a mortgage late, which is the worst type of late to have. Ultimately if the account is not brought current, it may report as a foreclosure. It is a very frustrating situation. In fact there are advertisements out there that say, "Save 70% on a timeshare by buying foreclosed." This is a situation that everyone needs to be aware of prior to entering into any type of contract on a timeshare.

Credit Cards

Did you know that when you charge a hotel or rental car to your credit card a "hold" will be placed on your card for a specific amount of money? The "hold" is often several times more than what you will be paying for that room or car. Since there could be higher charges than what you originally agreed to (room service at a hotel, late return of the rental car, etc.) they initially charge a higher amount to cover these possibilities. Once you have completed your transaction the "hold" amount is removed and you are charged for the final bill. This process can take days. Be careful that you are not relying on just one card while traveling as it may be possible to reach your credit limit while a "hold" is in effect. Even worse would be if a "hold" was placed on your debit card and it caused checks to bounce. Most companies will tell you how much of a "hold" they have placed on your card if you ask.

Divorce

Interestingly enough, the #1 cause of divorce is financial issues. It is not surprising to find out that divorce also has a severe impact on wealth. According to Jay Zagorsky, a research scientist at the Ohio State University's Center for Human Resource Research, divorced individuals experience a wealth drop of 77%. A key reason is that the consumption needs of two adults living together are less than the consumption needs of two separate single adult households. Zagorsky also notes that divorce causes many individuals to reduce their income earning efforts.

Obviously, divorce can have a major impact on credit. At some point in most marriages there are going to be accounts that are joint. Joint accounts pose the largest risk in a divorce. In most cases one spouse will be required to pay off an account leaving the other spouse not responsible for the debt. However, if it is a joint debt, in the eyes of the creditor it still belongs to both individuals. Here is an example:

John and Debbie just got divorced and John was awarded three credit cards in the divorce decree. The accounts are joint and therefore show up on both John and Debbie's credit reports. John decides he can't afford to make payments and doesn't pay. The late payments show up on Debbie's credit report. If John were to not make payments for several months the account could go to charge-off status and the entire balance would become past due. This could ruin Debbie's credit. Legally Debbie does not have to pay the debt, but from a credit reporting standpoint she is still liable for the actions of her ex-husband in regards to the credit cards because the accounts were jointly held.

Anytime someone is getting a divorce it is important that they make sure joint accounts are addressed to be paid and closed in the shortest period of time possible. Until the accounts are closed and paid in full there is always the possibility of negative influence from the ex-spouse.

I have witnessed this firsthand with my clients. Most divorces arise out of financial strife. Once the decree has been handed down by the judge it is typically not the end of the financial turmoil and many times it is just another chapter in an ongoing struggle. I have had clients who have decided to pay debts in full with their own money rather than let their ex-spouse ruin their credit. On the other end of the spectrum I have had clients who thought because they have a divorce decree none of this would be an issue. It is a very big issue, and an issue that everyone should be aware of.

In the case of a joint mortgage there are two options, sell the house or have it refinanced into the name of the spouse keeping the house. If neither option is possible do not take your name off of title with a quit-claim deed. If you are still on the mortgage there is a responsibility to the debt until it is paid in full, either by sale, refinance, or paid off in cash. Removing yourself from ownership is not a good idea since you still have a stake in it until the mortgage is paid in full. Notify the lender of your new address and request that a monthly statement be sent to you. Make sure you stay abreast that the payments are being made on-time. In regards to a car loan, follow the same procedure as a mortgage.

In terms of credit cards keep a watchful eye on these accounts. Under law, a creditor cannot close a joint account because of a change of marital status. Although they can do so at the request of either spouse. And while a joint credit card may be closed, it still has life until the balance is paid off. A closed credit card will still report each month as far as the payment history and the remaining balance.

Requesting a joint account be made individual does not guarantee the creditor will do so. They will require the individual to qualify on their own based on a new application. If the account has already fallen behind the creditor would rather have two people held responsible than just one. If the spouse responsible for the debt does not make payments the creditor will hope the other spouse will get tired of negative impact on their credit and just go ahead and pay it themselves.

If something like this were to happen, what recourse would you have? Very little, unfortunately. Only time will heal the damage done in most cases. However, there are some alternatives in moving forward. If you believe paying the debts in full on your own is in your best interest, request the creditor to remove the late payments based on paying off the balance. This may work in some cases based on the fact that the account was no longer your legal responsibility. Not every creditor will be willing to do this, but is certainly worth asking. If you have a divorce decree that shows you do not owe specific debts that have been late or past due on your credit report there are mortgage programs that will not penalize you for the downturn in the credit scores. Most programs that are manually underwritten will be able to take into consideration that you are no longer legally obligated to those debts awarded to an ex-spouse. The key to this working is that everything else must be perfect. Any debts that you are obligated to pay must be on time in order for an underwriter to consider approving the loan. There may be exceptions if something was late several years ago or there was a good reason something may have been late (i.e. ex-spouse disappeared with all the money in the bank account and you have documentation to support this).

The best thing to do is to assess your current situation. Now that the divorce is final, how many accounts do you have open in your name exclusively? Is there a good base of credit open and active or are we starting from scratch (everything was joint and had to be closed)? I highly encourage people to not open every account jointly with their spouse. There are too many variables in life and if you ever find yourself in a divorce situation the last thing you need is to be starting from scratch financially. Even if it is just a couple department store cards or a gas card, keep something in your name alone.

If we are starting from scratch the first thing to do is talk to friends or relatives to see if they would be willing to add you on to their credit cards as an authorized user. At least until you can get back on your feet. This will jumpstart your credit and will likely open the door to applying for credit cards in your own name. Keep in mind that it will take at least seven years for the new credit cards to age to the point of creating an extremely strong base. It won't necessarily take that long to get your credit scores to be good, depending whether any damage was done during the divorce proceedings or afterward.

Get a checking account established in your name alone. Make sure your car insurance, utilities, and cell phone are in your name exclusively. You want to make sure you are getting credit for everything you are paying out in case you need to rely upon alternative credit.

Speaking of alternative credit, you will also want to keep a close eye on utility bills, cable, etc. leading up to the divorce becoming final. I have had situations where the spouse who typically pays these bills decides not to pay them anymore. A few months later collections start popping up from the services that go unpaid. Take every precaution to check to make sure payments are being received. These often go unchecked. Divorce decrees do not address who is responsible for payment. Since they may pop up after the divorce is final it will remain an obligation for both parties until paid in full.

Your credit does not have to suffer during a divorce if you are proactive. Don't forget that as a joint borrower you can check on the account and make sure payment has been received. I would recommend doing this. If you can afford to make a payment when it is apparent your ex-spouse is dropping the ball, do it. It will ultimately be less painful knowing you saved your credit score and did not allow the ex-spouse the chance to hurt you financially down the road.

Co-signing

When you co-sign on a loan you are equally liable (along with the primary borrower) to repay the loan. A common co-signing situation is when a parent helps out a child by co-signing in order for a loan to be approved. Keep in mind that this debt will appear on the credit report and will have the same ramifications as if it were your debt exclusively. If you have co-signed for someone and they are 30 days late on the payment, it will hurt both of your credit scores. I have had many shocked and surprised parents in my office that cannot believe little Johnny or Sally was late on a loan they co-signed for.

Another cause for concern is co-signing on a credit card. Not only is there the risk of a late payment, but there should also be major concern for the balance on the card. If the card is maxed out, there will be a negative impact on credit scores. There is a certain unknown anytime you co-sign with someone. The only true precaution that can be taken (other than declining to co-sign) is to pay the bill yourself each month. It is a good thing to help your children get established in the world of credit. However, it is equally important to protect yourself.

106

If you do decide to co-sign, take the risk out of it by collecting the payment from the party that needed you in the first place and pay it yourself. The best way to do this is to have them write a check out directly to the lender and you mail it out yourself. This is especially helpful when you are trying to qualify for a new mortgage. If you can prove that full payment for the debt is coming from the other party's checking account, you may be able to exclude the monthly debt when qualifying for a mortgage. Depending on the size of the debt it could make a difference. Whereas if you receive the payment from the other party and then write a check yourself then it would appear that the other party is not solely responsible for the payment of the debt. By making sure the payment is going out each month you can rest assured there will not be a surprise the next time you are sitting in a lender's office applying for a loan. The only risk you would run at this point would be if the check were to bounce. At least under those circumstances you would still be well within 30 days of the due date to make the payment yourself if the other party was unable to make payment. When it comes to protecting our credit, co-signing is one of the biggest breaches of our security out there. We assume the other person is making the payments when they are due, but can you really be sure?

According to a 1992 Federal Trade Commission report, studies have shown that three out of four co-signers on defaulted loans ultimately repay the loan for the original borrower. Not very good odds to roll the dice on.

***

It is one thing to co-sign for someone because they have no credit. It is an entirely different thing to co-sign for someone because they have bad credit. If you are asked to co-sign for someone because their credit is less than favorable, BEWARE. History often repeats itself. This is a situation where you would absolutely want to send the payments out yourself each month.

In making the payments it is important to make sure it is paid by personal check. This gives you the best evidence in showing the payment was made by the other party, from their account. Paying by cash or money order does not provide a history to call upon if needed. It also does not show when the funds were received by the lender. If an issue came up regarding when the payment was received, personal checks show the date it was deposited by the lender. This may seem petty, but cancelled checks have been the key to many approvals over the years. Whether it was from allowing a debt to be excluded in qualifying, or it was evidence of when a lender received payment. Cancelled checks can be a great source of evidence for various reasons.

Student Loans

Did you hear about the executive who was recently arrested for embezzling $100,000 to pay for his daughter's college education? As the policeman, who also had a daughter in college, was leading him away in handcuffs, he said to the executive, "I have just one question for you. Where were you going to get the rest of the money?"

Student loans are a necessary thing for many people. Once we get out of the womb of college, reality hits us right in the face: These things have to be paid!!! For the typical government-backed student loan you cannot even file bankruptcy to avoid paying it back. In fact there are only two ways to get rid of federal student loan debt without paying it back: your death or your total and permanent disability. There are a few other possibilities, such as teaching in a designated low income school, but filing bankruptcy will not work.

For those having trouble meeting the obligation of a student loan, forbearance is an option. A forbearance is typically granted in 12 month increments to either reduce payment amounts or suspend payments completely. This can be renewed for up to three years. It generally requires evidence of economic hardship, but it is not a difficult thing to prove. If you are in the process of applying for a position in your field of study this is typically an acceptable reason. Many graduates end up with a lower paying job after graduation before they find something permanent in their field.

It is important to get a past due loan into forbearance status as quickly as possible. Once it is in default there is no opportunity to be granted a forbearance. Did you know that if you have been late on your payments it may be possible to get rid of the lates? Request that the lender back-date the forbearance to delete the late payments. Most lenders will do this for the previous 12 months. This really saves your credit and gives you an opportunity to get back on your feet.

Other ways for postponing student loan repayment:
- Returning to school at least half time
- Participating in an approved graduate fellowship
- Seeking but unable to find full-time employment

Pay Day Loans

Got a case of the shorts? The payday loan industry has taken the country by storm in the form of "easy money." You go into a location, fill out an application, give identification, maybe your employment is verified, write a check for a couple hundred dollars and out the door you go with cash in hand…and so the cycle begins. Payday loans create a dependency for constant cash infusions. The cost to get that infusion is monumental.

The numbers are sobering when we take a look: Jake borrows $200 for a two week term. He is charged $30 for the loan, which equals 15% interest. This breaks down to 7.5% per week. But if Jake can't pay off that loan, and takes a full year to pay it back, he would be looking at 7.5% for 52.14 weeks and that means 391.07% annual percentage rate (APR)!

***

Payday loans are meant to be short term loans, and short term loans come at a higher cost. When it turns into a long term loan the cost becomes alarming.

Pay Day Tax Loans

Refund anticipation loans (RAL) are a variation of the pay day loan. A taxpayer is due a refund from the IRS, so the tax preparer offers the money immediately for a fee. Partnering with lending institutions, tax preparers across the country offer this service. Based on information from the IRS, the National Consumer Law Center (NCLC) and Consumer Federation of America (CFA) estimate 12.38 million Americans used RALs in 2004. This was at a cost of $1.6 billion.

The refund loan only has a life of a couple weeks in most cases. Since the loan is so short term the cost to do it is extremely high. If someone were to get a refund of $2,000 at a cost of $100 they would be paying 5% of the loan amount. However, if you base it on the annual percentage rate (APR) it would be over 130%. Is this somewhat misleading? Perhaps.

Since the loan is only for a couple weeks and not for a full year, the tax payer is only paying $100. 130% APR on $2,000 would mean $2,607 ($50 multiplied by 52.14 weeks) in fees. This is not the case as the loan is paid off quickly.

I have encountered situations where a RAL turns into a real monster. I have had clients with collections based on an expected tax refund. Ultimately their refund was less than the amount they were loaned. Many of these clients claimed they were shown the higher refund amount and then it was switched to a lower amount before being submitted to the IRS. This is a case of activity that the FTC needs to be alerted to. Situations like this are rare and I would say 99% of tax preparers would not do this, but the 1% that does usually preys on the most desperate of people who may never say anything. There are situations where this could unintentionally occur. The IRS may deny the refund, a taxpayer may need to amend the taxes unexpectedly, past due child support could prevent the receipt of a refund, etc. You may want to avoid these loans and just wait a couple weeks for your tax refund since these loans involve many variables out of your control.

One of the nation's largest tax preparers settled on a series of lawsuits filed for its practice of promoting RALs. In December 2005 the settlement was announced, but the terms were not disclosed. The payout of claims will go to 8

million customers who took out loans between 1989 and 2005. In a statement the tax preparer said it would have to incur a tax charge of $31 million to cover the claims. That amounts to $3.88 for each customer, minus attorney's fees.

***

Wise Moves for Credit Cards

I am a firm believer in the school of thought that a vast majority of Americans are in over their heads with credit card debt. Earlier in the book I discussed the catchy advertising the credit card company's use; it's in our heads. It is convenient, it's there, it is available and it is everywhere. For those of you who do not have credit card debt...congratulations. Keep the cards open and use them as a tool to keep your credit scores high. I have said repeatedly that credit cards are our best source for making sure our credit scores are high. This is only true if we manage them well.

For those enslaved by credit card debt, we need to have a little heart to heart discussion. I think for each and everyone one of us in the back of our mind we tell ourselves "this isn't forever, I will pay this off." When? Most of us have a 401(k), an IRA or some other form of retirement account. The historical annual rate of return is 8% - 10%. We can expect to earn somewhere in that range on our money. Yet we pay anywhere from 16% - 29% on the money we borrow from credit cards. Do you see the gross difference in what we typically earn on our own money versus the cost of the money we are borrowing? Most people think they need to just have more money to pay toward the debt in order to get out from underneath it. Not true. More money to apply toward debt is good, but is not necessary to shorten the time it takes to pay a debt off. A software company in Austin, TX called ARC Systems® has come up with software that dissects the credit card payment process. The dissection of the process shows a consumer how to knock out the debt faster without necessarily paying more money. Who wouldn't want to pay down debt faster without more out of pocket? Only gluttons for punishment I suppose. They have an excellent feature called the "Education Wizard," which gives you a full understanding of how credit card payments really work. Check it out for yourself at www.DebtLogistics.com. When you think about the depression, discord and sleepless nights credit card debt has caused so many people, the time to address the problem is now and a solution exists. Let me just say one last thing on this topic: If you are paying 0% on a balance transfer on a card you had a previous balance on you are likely in a negative amortization situation. This means that you are actually accumulating more debt from interest on the original balance than what you are paying monthly in most cases. Go see what the experts at Debt Logistics™ have to say about this. On the website (www.DebtLogistics.com) be sure to enter the promotional code 'creditroadmap' after you have filled in your personal information. You can also list me (Patrick Ritchie) as the person who referred you.

- Always pay more than the minimum payment. If you get in the habit of paying only the minimum it will become just that, a habit. Paying the minimum each month will cost a lot more in the long run in terms of more interest and the debt will typically continue to grow larger.
- Avoid cash advances on credit cards. The interest on cash advances is higher than the interest for a purchase. There is typically no grace period on cash advances, you start paying interest immediately.
- Watch your balance to limit ratio. You never want to have a balance greater than 50% of your limit. The lower the ratio the better. The best position is to stay at a zero balance or just limited use.

- Avoid applying to all of the pre-approved offers you receive. You should accumulate credit cards slowly over time; never apply for several in a short timeframe.
- Make your payments on-time. Making payments late is one of the worst things you can do in regards to credit. Not only will it hurt your credit if you are 30 days late, but it can cost you money in fees and an increase in your interest rate. If you realize your credit card is due today make a call to the company and do a payment by phone. Keep in mind that credit card companies could have a specific time of the day that the payment must be received by to post that day, so call early. You may be charged to make a payment by phone, but it could be less than what the late fee would be.

Credit warning signs:
- You are late making payments
- You always pay the minimum only
- You are at the credit limit or have exceeded it
- You are using one credit card to pay off another
- You are losing sleep at night because of your debts
- Your entire check goes to pay bills and you can only buy necessities using a credit card

***

RECAP

- By calling 1-888-567-8688 and opting out, you can save yourself the headache of receiving "pre-approved" offers.
- Beware of setting up automated payments. Always make sure the payments are being made and being made on time. You will also want to confirm that the bank is not mistakenly making more than one payment or paying out more money than you authorized.
- Avoid store financing and those offers at the cash register to "save 10%" on that day's purchases. Financing furniture and other items using store incentives such as the "90 day same as cash" deal can negatively impact your credit – showing as a maxed out account on your report.
- Beware of timeshares. They appear as real estate on your credit report and if you fail to make payments, it can appear as a foreclosure and ruin your credit.
- Protect your credit from medical collections by staying on top of the insurance company and making sure that payment is being made. It's easy for things to slip between the cracks and end in collection later. Stay in close communication with the medical billing department and the insurance company to make sure all information is correct and things are moving along.
- In the case of a divorce, make sure you are aware of all the accounts held in both your names and make sure that you stay informed, even if your spouse (ex-spouse) is supposedly paying the bill. Establish a checking account in your name only and stay on top of your utility, cell phone and other payments, as you will most likely need alternative credit as you re-establish your credit as an individual, separate from your spouse.
- If you decide to co-sign, make sure payments are being made. Have the co-borrower make the payment

out to the lender via check, but hand it over to you each month for mailing. This way you know the payment is being sent out.

- Don't let student loans go into default. You have options such as deferments and forbearance if you have trouble meeting your obligation for the time being. It is important to do this <u>before</u> the loan goes into default.
- Avoid Pay Day and early Tax Refund loans. The interest on these loans are astronomical and can land you in hot water if you find yourself with an inability to pay them off.

***

Chapter 6

Credit Fact or Fiction

"Facts do not cease to exist because they are ignored."
- Aldous Huxley

A key aspect of your credit score is the ratio of your debts to your assets.
Fiction. Credit scores do not consider our assets; our checking and savings balances are not reported to credit bureaus. A credit report contains no knowledge of assets whatsoever, therefore it could not calculate a ratio of debts to assets in the credit scores. There could be confusion of a different ratio as there is definitely a calculation of existing balances to available credit on revolving accounts, and this does play a key role in our credit scores.

"Charge-off" means you do not have to worry about the debt.
Fiction. When an account is in charge-off status it means the original creditor has written the debt off of its books. The past due amount will most likely end up with a collection agency at some point. The debt is still owed until it is paid unless it was included in a bankruptcy.

Closing accounts will remove the late payments on an account.
Fiction. Closing an account does not change the history of the account. In fact it is always better to leave an account

117

open, especially in the case of revolving debt. Once a credit card account is closed you are no longer a customer of that institution. If you keep the account open and remain a customer you will have more negotiating power in the future. A single late payment may be removed by the creditor if you ask or are able to demonstrate that you made a good faith effort to get the payment sent in, but extenuating circumstances prevented it from taking place.

The best thing I can do for my credit is to payoff my credit cards and close them.
Fiction. When you close your credit cards you are ending the positive history that is flowing into your credit report each month from these accounts. Eliminating this flow of information can hurt the credit score in the future. Since credit cards are such a powerful tool in boosting and maintaining high credit scores, it is imperative to keep these types of accounts open forever. The longer they are open the more positive impact they will provide to the scores. Assuming the payments are on time and the balances are under 50% of the available limit, credit cards are the most powerful tool in maintaining excellent credit scores. Consumers who close credit card accounts may have to completely rebuild their credit history.

It is up to me to inform my student loan lenders if I am continuing my education and keeping my loans in deferment.
Fact. It is very common for students who are continuing their education to later find out their student loans reported as being late when they assumed there was no payment due because they were still in school full-time. Keep communication open with student loan companies to make sure they have accurate information regarding your graduation date and your payment status. If you have graduated and are unable to meet the obligation for the monthly student loan payment, request a forbearance

118

postponing your payments so that you do not have late payments appear for your account.

Using a debit card is a good way to build a credit history.
Fiction. Debit cards do not report to the credit bureaus. You are not borrowing money when a debit card is used. Since you are using your own funds this is not something that is going to be reported as an account on your credit report.

A divorce decree will help me clear up negative things on my credit report.
Fiction. A divorce decree can demonstrate whether you are legally liable for a particular debt, but it will not remove information pertaining to that debt from your credit report. If your ex-spouse is responsible for a particular account according to the divorce decree you are still open to the payment performance of that account. If the payments are late or not made at all this will impact your credit scores if you were on the account jointly.

Credit scoring considers age, income and occupation.
Fiction. Although credit scoring is a statistical profile of potential consumer stability, age, income and occupation are not factors in credit scores. Nowhere on the credit report does it list the income of a consumer. Often the birthdates and occupations are incorrect on credit reports. Both pieces of information are considered neutral as they do not factor into the modern day scoring model.

If I am denied credit this will be reported and hurt my credit.
Fiction. If you are denied credit this will not be reported to the credit bureaus. You will receive notice that your application could not be granted, but there is no place on the credit report where this is recorded. The only record of the application would be the inquiry of the creditor pulling

119

your credit report. The inquiry itself does not distinguish whether credit was extended as a result of the application. The only way it would be known is if an account eventually was reported on the credit report. Denied loans have no history or impact when it comes to credit reports and scores.

Credit bureaus approve and deny loans.
Fiction. The credit bureaus do not make lending decisions. They merely act as third party information providers. The information the bureaus will provide to lenders and other entities includes:
- Identification and possibly employment data
- Payment history
- Public records (consumer related)
- Inquiries showing other credit applications

Even if you have a zero balance on a credit card you will be hit with potential debt.
Fiction. Years ago on government mortgages they would add $10 as a payment on a zero balance line of credit. That is no longer the case. In fact, having credit available and managing it well is like the proverbial carrot dangling in front of us. If it is there and we have not abused it the likelihood that we would abuse it in the future is less. Credit card companies may be less likely to grant further unsecured debt to someone who already has a lot available, but this is not the case for secured debt such as a home or car.

Credit scores are a grade of past credit behavior.
Fiction. Credit scores are actually a prediction of future credit behavior, namely the likelihood of being repaid by the consumer in question. Though credit scores are based on past behavior they are designed to predict our future financial responsibility. This explains why a late payment this month would have a greater adverse impact than a late

payment from many years ago. If your credit card balance was maxed out three months ago the credit scores do not take that into consideration. Your most recent balances would be taken into consideration since it is the most recent display of your likelihood to repay a debt tomorrow.

You are not responsible for debts on a joint credit card if you did not sign for the purchase.
Fiction. As a joint borrower on a credit card, or any account, you are responsible for the activity of the account. With this being the case it is imperative to only co-sign with people you trust completely.

Your salary/income impacts your credit score.
Fiction. There is no area of the credit report that lists income or even a range of income. Your income does not have any influence over your credit score. However, your income is considered when applying for a loan and is generally one of the aspects of an approval. The credit score itself is just one aspect of an approval, just as income, employment, down payment and assets would be.

When you are married your credit report merges with your spouse.
Fiction. This is not true, yet I hear people talk about it all the time. Once you are married a credit report may be pulled jointly with your spouse. However, your accounts will still be separated according to what accounts you originally signed for. Only joint accounts are the responsibility of both spouses. There may be some exceptions to liability in community property states, but this would not be something that would appear on the credit report. Your credit scores are based solely on the accounts that belong to you. Late payments on a spouse's personal accounts will not impact your credit scores.

If I pay cash for everything this looks better than if I use credit.

Fiction. Paying cash will not reflect on the credit report. In fact, the person who only pays cash and does not have credit runs the risk of having no credit when they need it for a major purchase. I have had clients who for years only paid cash for everything. With no credit history this had a varying affect on their ability to get a mortgage. There will always be options for people with no bad credit whether they have a credit score or not. People who pay cash only and have had bad credit in the past run a greater risk than those who always had good credit and choose to pay cash now. Bad credit needs good credit to offset it, whereas good credit just needs a little nudge of positive credit here and there to keep the flames going.

Credit scores can change frequently.

Fact. Credit scores are constantly changing, depending on what is being reported. Creditors report at various times of the month and this can mean scores will change accordingly. If there are no major changes such as a late payment or a collection it is unlikely the scores will vary by much. For someone who does the same thing each month there may be little change at all. Paying a balance off in full after carrying a large balance for a few months could have a significantly positive effect on the credit scores from the previous months.

Despite the use of credit scores, the information contained in the credit report is still important in a lending decision.

Fact. Credit scores are certainly an important part of a lending decision, but the credit report is still looked at and given weight for what it contains. Someone who was late on an account, but still has high credit scores could be penalized by the existence of a recent late payment even if it did not throw the scores off dramatically. As important as

122

credit scores are, the nuts and bolts of the credit report are just as important overall.

C hapter 7

Repairing Credit

"Do not be desirous of having things done quickly. Do not look at small advantages. Desire to have things done quickly prevents their being done thoroughly. Looking at small advantages prevents great affairs from being accomplished." - *Confucius*

If you see that your name is misspelled, or your address or employment are incorrect, contact the credit bureaus. But if the inaccurate information involves more than just a misspelling or incorrect employer, it's time to initiate a dispute investigation. And it is best to launch an investigation with the credit bureaus as well as contact the creditor that reported.

You will write a letter detailing what is incorrect on your report (you can find an example in the back of this book). Once you have your letter written and your copies of supporting documentation, make sure you mail it out to all three credit bureaus. Since the credit bureaus receive numerous disputes, it is recommended to send it Certified Mail. Now you have documentation that your dispute was received.

When the credit bureaus receive a dispute they will contact the creditor that reported the information in the first place.

Once contacted, the original creditor has 30 days to respond. There are three possibilities from this point:

- The original creditor agrees with the dispute. The incorrect information will be removed.
- The original creditor disagrees with the dispute. The information will remain on the report. From this point a consumer would need to go directly to the creditor to argue the point of concern.
- The original creditor does not respond to the credit bureau. The information must be removed.

Once a dispute investigation has concluded, the credit bureaus will send a copy of the credit report. This will happen whether the information was corrected or not. For any consumer making a dispute, they should know that the dispute investigation is not over until the revised credit report (which is free) has been received. It is not uncommon for information to be corrected by two credit bureaus but not the third. In this situation repeat the process and note that the other two credit bureaus have already corrected the information. Now you are only disputing with the remaining credit bureau, not all three.

Re-aging Accounts

There is a way to get rid of late payments on credit cards that were in fact late. Re-aging is a method in which a creditor will erase past transgressions under guidelines set forth under the Uniform Retail Credit Classification and Account Management Policy published by the Federal Financial Institutions Examination Council in June 2000. Essentially it is possible to remove a few past late payments if you fall within the guidelines:

- Borrower demonstrates a willingness and ability to pay.

- The credit card account should be at least 9 months old.
- The borrower must make at least three payments of the minimum required payment or the equivalent amount.
- A creditor may only re-age an account once in a 12-month period and twice in a five-year period.

Whether or not a creditor will re-age your account is at the sole discretion of the creditor. There is no requirement for creditors to re-age accounts; simply, there are guidelines to follow in re-aging. Contact your creditors for their policy regarding re-aging.

Your Personal Statement

You have the right to add a 100-word statement to an account that you are disputing or that has been determined to be accurate, yet you disagree. The statement will tell your side of the story. However, it will not impact your credit score either positively or negatively. It is important to make sure the statement is clear and concise. Pretend you are speaking to a judge who is going to render a decision of your guilt or innocence. If your explanation points toward the fact that you just do not want to pay the claim, you would be better off not adding this to your credit report. Here are some examples:

Good: *"This account belongs to someone with a different social security number."*

An underwriter would likely be willing to hear the entire story and accept evidence that the account did not match your social security number.

Bad: *"I have attempted to resolve this collection, but they are not willing to work with me."*

126

An underwriter would assume that the debt must be owed since the statement does not clearly say the account does not belong to the consumer. From the statement it appears the consumer is trying to pay less than the full amount owed.

It is a good idea to have someone else review your statement prior to adding it to your credit report. Just because it makes sense to you does not mean everyone will interpret the statement in the same way. The example of a bad statement could very easily be the same situation as the good example, but it is not clear why the collection needs to be resolved, other than being paid. Be specific and factual. Rambling on and making allegations is not a good approach.

The Bad Debt Market

The debt buying industry is a multi-billion dollar industry. Credit card charge-offs and other bad debt hovers around $65 billion a year according to *Nilson Report*, a consumer credit newsletter. Once lenders stop attempts to collect bad debts internally, the debts are typically sold in bundles to companies that specialize in the bad debt market. Bad debts are often sold for pennies on the dollar. However, a bad debt portfolio will typically go for $1 million to $2 million. These companies weed out the debts that were included in bankruptcy or are otherwise uncollectible. Then the debts are packaged for resale to collection agencies and lawyers.

In some cases consumers are contacted by collectors regarding debts older than seven years. Debts this old are not enforceable in court. Nor are they reportable to credit bureaus. Be careful, if you make a payment you could reset the statute of limitations or reset the timeframe on the seven year rule for reporting to credit bureaus.

The FTC went after NCO Group for reporting collection accounts using later-than-actual delinquency dates. In changing the date of delinquency it could cause a debt to be reported beyond the seven year limit allowed. For example, if the original debt was reported delinquent in 12/03 and changed to 12/05 it would extend the reporting of the debt for another two years beyond what is legally allowed. To settle the charges NCO Group has to pay $1,500,000. According to NCO Group it had obtained bad information about the age of the debts from a creditor. NCO Group is the largest debt collector in the world. Situations such as this show why it is important to save paperwork and keep copies of your past credit reports. You may have to prove dates are being reported incorrectly at some point.

***

There is a new collection philosophy and it's all about being nice. It involves:

- Moving from tough, threatening tactics to a customer service methodology
- Treating debtors with respect
- Asking questions with a focus on solving the underlying delinquency problem
- Being firm but fair
- Flexibility in negotiating repayment
- Really listening
- Pre-empting competition for payment dollars by focusing on early stage delinquency

Charge-off Accounts

A charge-off will typically be associated with an unsecured debt such as a credit card. If payment is not received after a certain number of months, the lender will write off the debt as "unreceivable." <u>This does not mean the debt has been forgiven.</u>

I want to make it very clear that a charge-off does not mean the debt is no longer owed. I have had several people come into my office and tell me the charge-off is not owed. Charge-off is just the technical term; it is still a past due amount. When someone is in charge-off status, they do have some negotiating possibilities. Keep in mind that the charge-off will show as past due on the credit report until:

- It is paid in full, then it will need to be updated reflecting paid in full.

<u>or</u>

- 7 years have passed from the negative date

<u>or</u>

- It is included in a bankruptcy or payment plan such as consumer credit counseling

Once an account has been charged off, it will generally go to collection. This is when the problems start on the credit report.

ABC Credit Company charges-off $500. Then the uncollectible debt is turned over to XYZ Collection Agency. Now the consumer shows a past due amount with ABC Credit Company for $500. Even though it has been charged-off, it is still owed and shows as being past due. There will now be a second reporting of the same debt from XYZ Collection Agency showing $500 owed and past due. This is where the debt begins to snowball because on the credit report it looks like two different accounts, each owing $500 and past due. The first collection agency will *only try for so long before a second or third collection company may show up on the credit report. It is not uncommon to see the same debt show up two, three or even four times or more under different accounts. The reality of this is that the debt should only be reported once under the company most recently attempting to collect the money. What actually happens is that as the debt moves from company to company, the previous company does not go back to update what they reported. A consumer needs to be aware of this and dispute any old tradelines of a past due amount being collected by a new company.*

If you ever have a charge-off or a collection, be sure to go back and clean up the mess left from previous collectors for the debt.

If you do want to pay it and get it out of your hair, offer to pay half. You may have to pay whoever is currently collecting the debt rather than the original creditor. This is not unusual. The most important thing is to pay with a personal check or credit card. Never settle a bad debt with a money order, cashier's check or cash. You need a record to show you paid it. A personal check is best because it must be endorsed by whoever it is written to. Once you have made your settlement, be sure to get a paid statement reflecting a $0 balance. It is wise to get the terms of your settlement in writing prior to paying anything. Once you do receive a paid in full statement, put it in a safe place. If the debt ever shows back up on your credit report you will need evidence to show it was paid. Otherwise you may end up paying the same debt twice to clear it up.

Settling Collections

All collection agencies and creditors are willing to settle for less than the full balance. The exception to this would be student loans. Student loans are backed by the government, so there is no settling and student loans cannot be discharged in a bankruptcy.

The average settlement would be anywhere from 35% to 65% of the full balance owed. This will vary from company to company depending on their guidelines for settling.

Paying or settling a collection or charge-off will not delete it from the credit report. It will need to be updated as being "paid in full" or "settled." The benefit is that it will no longer show as a past due amount. The derogatory account will stay on the credit report for seven years from the date it initially became delinquent.

It is worth paying a collection in full if the agency is willing to remove it completely from the credit report. However, this is not very likely, especially because there may be several parties involved. Just because the collection agency may agree to remove the account completely does not mean the original creditor will be willing to do so, nor any previous collection agencies that attempted to get payment. For a straight collection, such as medical, there is a much stronger possibility. In the case of charged-off accounts from credit card companies this is not likely.

Once a collection is four years old it has less impact on the credit score. Beware when you are close to making a major purchase. If you have a credit score that meets the requirement of a loan it is best not to pay a collection until instructed to do so by your lender (which may not be until the loan is closing). The reason for this is that as soon as payment is made the account will reflect the most recent date of activity and may no longer be viewed as an old account having less effect on the credit scores. With the more recent date from paying it off the credit scoring will think it is a recent account and may drop the scores. This is less of a concern if you are not about to make a major purchase within the next six months or so.

***

Why do unpaid collections get reported on a specific date and then may go years without being reported as a current collection? It costs money to report to the credit bureaus and it would not typically be cost effective for a collection agency to report the past due amount each month. Because of this many collections will appear to be old, but in reality they are still currently past due.

It is best to pay a collection as soon as you are aware of it. There are a few reasons for this. First of all, paying it off will at least allow you to have the account reflect as a zero balance and start aging from that point. This way you are not going to have to be concerned with going back and paying after years have passed and making it reflect as a more recent derogatory account when it is paid. Secondly, a collection agency may sue and get a judgment for the balance. Going to court costs money, however. So this typically happens when large amounts of money are in question. In this situation the consumer would have a collection and a judgment showing for the same account. Thirdly, collections may be sold several times over. So the same debt can show up multiple times on the credit report.

Do not make a payment on a derogatory account that you do not intend to pay in full or are in the process of settling. Many times a collection agency may call a consumer to coax them into making a small payment toward the debt. They may tell the consumer that this will buy them some time to pay off the rest of the amount. The reality is that by making any amount of payment will reset the clock for how long it can be reported. More importantly it will reset the statute of limitations for being sued over the debt.

Credit Counseling

Credit counseling has helped numerous people get out from under the burden of severe debt. I would say it is a viable option for people. However, in going the credit counseling route it is important to know who you are dealing with. Look for an agency that is a member of the National Foundation of Consumer Counseling. Go to www.debtadvice.org and you will be provided with an affiliate of the NFCC in your area.

There is no federal regulation of debt counseling services. With this being the case you need to watch out for what services you become involved with. Here are some things to know:

- Avoid any company that advertises on TV or that specifically solicits you (may be from a pre-screened list)
- Non-profit is a meaningless designation
- Never believe that your debt can be wiped out

The IRS has and is currently considering revoking the non-profit status of some credit counseling agencies. The cases of those being revoked would be forwarded to the Department of Justice for prosecution. One investigation revealed the income of a founder of a non-profit counseling agency as being $624,000 annually.

Credit Counseling vs. Debt Settlement

There is a difference between credit counseling and debt settlement. Most of the advertisements we see and hear about addressing credit problems are coming from debt settlement companies. You make payments to the company

133

and in return your money is held. Once the credit gets to the point where creditors believe the debts will never be repaid, the settlement comes in. This results in a major blow to the credit of a consumer.

One thing consumers need to know is that anytime they settle an account for less than what was owed there is a strong likelihood that the debt will be reported as income on a 1099 for the year the settlement took place. If a consumer owed $10,000 and settled for $5,000 they would likely receive a 1099 for $5,000 in income from the amount of the original debt that was forgiven. In some cases a debt settlement company might keep all money paid into the plan if a consumer misses a payment or decides to leave the program.

Credit Repair Organizations

Congressional research has found that:

(1) Consumers have a vital interest in establishing and maintaining their credit worthiness and credit standing in order to obtain and use credit. As a result, consumers who have experienced credit problems may seek assistance from credit repair organizations which offer to improve the credit standing of such consumers.

(2) Certain advertising and business practices of some companies engaged in the business of credit repair services have worked a financial hardship upon consumers, particularly those of limited economic means and who are inexperienced in credit matters.

Credit Repair Organizations (CROs) may not charge or receive any money before any services promised to the consumer have been performed. Also, a CRO should provide the following statement before any agreement is performed:

134

Consumer Credit File Rights Under State and Federal Law

You have a right to dispute inaccurate information in your credit report by contacting the credit bureau directly. However, neither you nor any "credit repair" company or credit repair organization has the right to have accurate, current, and verifiable information removed from your credit report. The credit bureau must remove accurate, negative information from your report only if it is over 7 years old. Bankruptcy information can be reported for 10 years.

You have a right to obtain a copy of your credit report from a credit bureau. You may be charged a reasonable fee. There is no fee, however, if you have been turned down for credit, employment, insurance, or a rental dwelling because of information in your credit report within the preceding 60 days. The credit bureau must provide someone to help you interpret the information in your credit file. You are entitled to receive a free copy of your credit report if you are unemployed and intend to apply for employment in the next 60 days, if you are a recipient of public welfare assistance, or if you have reason to believe that there is inaccurate information in your credit report due to fraud.

You have a right to sue a credit repair organization that violates the Credit Repair Organization Act. This law prohibits deceptive practices by credit repair organizations.

You have the right to cancel your contract with any credit repair organization for any reason within 3 business days from the date you signed it.

Credit bureaus are required to follow reasonable procedures to ensure that the information they report is accurate. However, mistakes may occur.

You may, on your own, notify a credit bureau in writing that you dispute the accuracy of information in your credit file. The credit bureau must then reinvestigate and modify or remove inaccurate or incomplete information. The credit bureau may not charge any fee for this service. Any pertinent information and copies of all documents you have concerning an error should be given to the credit bureau.

If the credit bureau's reinvestigation does not resolve the dispute to your satisfaction, you may send a brief statement to the credit bureau, to be kept in your file, explaining why you think the record is inaccurate. The credit bureau must include a summary of your statement about disputed information with any report it issues about you.

The Federal Trade Commission regulates credit bureaus and credit repair organizations. For more information contact:

The Public Reference Branch
Federal Trade Commission
Washington, D.C. 20580

This means CROs are under a tight rein in regards to what they can do for you and for the most part, you can take control of credit repair yourself.

- For erroneous information on your report such as a misspelled name, incorrect address, etc. contact the credit bureaus. For more in-depth investigations of inaccurate information, make sure you contact both the bureaus and the original creditor who reported the inaccurate information.

- You may add a 100 word statement to an account and submit it to the bureaus regarding a disagreement you have with something reported in your file. This statement will not have any impact on your scores.
- Charge-offs are debts that were never paid and are still owed. The debt has not been forgiven. You may settle a charge-off by offering to pay half or some amount of the debt. Always remember to settle the debt with a personal check or credit card and keep a receipt of payment. You will also want a statement from the creditor or collection agency that the debt has been settled. Once paid, the charge-off will remain on the credit report, but should be updated to reflect "paid."
- Pay a collection as soon as you become aware of it. You want your report to show the account at zero and that negative history to start aging as soon as possible so that it will have less impact on your scores. If you have an old collection and are within six months of financing a major purchase it is advisable to leave it alone until instructed to pay it off as part of your approval for the major purchase. Paying off old collection accounts could actually lower your credit scores rather than helping them.
- Do not make a payment on any derogatory account that you do not intend to pay in full or settle immediately. Once you make that payment, the clock gets reset in regards to the statute of limitations and repayment of an old debt.
- The average settlement on charge-offs and collections are between 35% to 65% of the balance owed.
- Research any credit counseling or credit repair organizations fully before signing any agreements or making any payments.

***

C hapter 8

Bankruptcy

"The gem cannot be polished without friction, nor man perfected without trials." - *Chinese Proverb*

Bankruptcy has been around for hundreds of years. The term bankruptcy comes from the Latin terms "Bancus," the tradesman's counter, and "Ruptus," broken; indicating a place of business was broken or gone. Thankfully, we no longer live in a time when creditors come and break our things to collect a debt.

The number of personal bankruptcies in the United States is approaching two million a year. That's twice as many as in 1995 and six times as many as in 1980. A 1997 study by Visa showed that almost half of bankruptcy decisions were attributed to aggressive collection tactics. Unemployment, medical expenses, divorce, local economic factors and other life events can lead people down the path of owing more than they are capable of repaying.

According to the American Bar Association, nearly 1/3 of bankruptcy filers owed an entire year's salary on their credit cards. Studies have also shown that 24 months prior to filing bankruptcy, balances typically double. From what I see in my office I would say this is generally true.

A common example of how things can spiral out of control:

Dwayne received a lot of medical bills not covered by insurance. Dwayne wants to pay what he owes, but he just doesn't have the cash. Dwayne decides to use his credit cards to pay off the medical charges. So now Dwayne's credit card balances go up and so do his minimum payments. Since Dwayne missed work during his medical crisis, his income has taken a hit as well. The next thing Dwayne knows the credit card bills have become unmanageable. He decides to take out a line of credit on his house. At this point Dwayne is hoping things get better, because if they don't, the house could be lost. Especially if more medical bills keep coming.

There have been changes made to Bankruptcy Law:

- Consumers will be required to obtain certified financial counseling at least 6 months prior to being eligible to file.
- Consumers must meet a "means test" to determine whether permission to discharge debt can be granted.
- Bankruptcy attorneys will be held liable for providing accurate financial information on their client.
- The "means test" replaces judicial discretion.
- A debtor who does not meet the "means test" for eligibility to discharge debts can still file for Chapter 13.
- Under the new law, the amount to be repaid in a Chapter 13 will likely be more than under the old law.

Chapter 7 (Debt Liquidation)

When someone files for bankruptcy there is generally a three month time frame before the bankruptcy is approved for discharge. The credit reporting clock starts ticking from the discharge date, not the filing date. Existing debts are discharged, which means the debt is no longer owed. Those debts that cannot be discharged in a bankruptcy include:

- Recent debts to the IRS
- Most alimony or child support orders
- Obligations owed as a result of criminal or fraudulent action
- Government backed student loans
- Court judgments resulting in damages due to driving while intoxicated

Some debts may be reaffirmed, which means the consumer will continue paying on the debt. Reaffirmed debts are excluded from the discharged debts. Many people who file for bankruptcy will reaffirm debts such as a mortgage or car loan. It depends on the current situation as to whether someone should consider reaffirming a debt. Here are some examples:

Jake has $100,000 in medical debts. He is able to handle his other obligations, such as his house payment and car payment. He has some small credit card debt. The $100,000 Jake owes for medical collections is an amount he just isn't able to repay. Jake files to discharge the $100,000 in medical debt, but reaffirm his other debts. By keeping the debts he can afford, he will be able to rebound from the bankruptcy quicker. By only discharging his medical debts Jake can get a FHA mortgage twelve months after the date of discharge.

Wanda also has $100,000 in medical debts. While she seems to make payments on her house and car just fine, Wanda decides to give herself a "clean slate" and includes her house and car loan in the bankruptcy. But now Wanda runs the risk of losing her home and car if she fails to *maintain payments. When a mortgage is included in a bankruptcy, as long as payments are still made, the house does not get foreclosed. However, the house and car would both be taken back if payments are not made.*

Daniel is also saddled with $100,000 in medical collections. When he files bankruptcy, he decides to add those pesky credit card accounts to give him some "breathing room." By adding consumer debt into his bankruptcy, Daniel gave his credit a big push into negative territory. Now Daniel will have to wait 24 months (a year longer than if he had gone with a straight medical bankruptcy) to be eligible for a FHA mortgage.

But Julie is in the worst position of all. While she too lives with $100,000 in medical debt, she decides to add her credit cards, her house and her car into the whole bankruptcy. Everything is included in that bankruptcy so she can start her new life. Only now Julie has put her new life into a very precarious position on two fronts. Julie will lose the house and the car if the payments are not made. And in terms of the credit score, she now has no accounts being paid on. With nothing positive on her credit report, Julie's credit scores will be low until she is able to re-establish her credit. By discharging everything, Julie is starting from scratch. Actually she will be starting from less than scratch because of the negatives from the bankruptcy.

Can someone get a mortgage a day out of bankruptcy? Yes. Is it feasible? Generally, no. Even though there are mortgage programs available for people a day out of bankruptcy, the requirements are often unrealistic. For a person with a large down payment it may be more realistic. A year after bankruptcy there are more programs available, albeit at a higher rate than a standard conventional mortgage. Of the mortgage programs that offer standard interest rates, FHA is the most lenient when it comes to a bankruptcy.

It is possible to get the scores back into an average range in a few years after a bankruptcy. This will vary according to what steps the consumer takes to restore the overall credit history. From the standpoint of FHA mortgage guidelines, when someone loses a house in a bankruptcy (foreclosure, whether due to a bankruptcy or not) they must wait 36 months before being eligible for a FHA mortgage. The bottom line is that there are different severities to a bankruptcy.

If you ever find yourself behind on your mortgage payment, take action. Never let the bank take it back. Sell the house before it becomes too late. When is it too late? Typically you would never want to get three months (90 days) behind on your mortgage payment. On paper, whether a house is taken back or not, 90 days past due equates as a foreclosure under some mortgage guidelines. Do not wait this long to take action. Although, if a settlement statement showing the sale of the home can be provided, some programs will not count it as a bankruptcy. By showing the house was sold prior to the finalization of a foreclosure this can be a saving grace when trying to buy a new house.

Chapter 13 (Wage Earner Plan)

This is generally considered less harsh than a Chapter 7, although from a credit score standpoint it could prolong the length of time accounts show as negative. A Bankruptcy Trustee (the court) works with the existing creditors to create a plan that allows a consumer to pay back debts. Typically the amount repaid is a lower amount than the amount showing owed. Interest and penalties may be substantially reduced. The lower amount is more manageable to repay and can sometimes cut the debt in half. The timeframe of repayment may be 1 to 4 years, but this will vary. Once the repayment is complete no creditor can come back and attempt to collect more.

Chapter 13 vs. Credit Counseling

The banking industry has always been torn in regards to both Chapter 13 bankruptcy and credit counseling. Which is a better solution? Is one worse than the other? Either way, a consumer has accepted that he is experiencing financial hardship and is seeking to remedy the situation. Banks always like it when borrowers make their best effort to repay what they owe.

A Chapter 13 involves a legally binding arrangement signed by a judge. It has some serious clout in terms of its requirements. A creditor cannot come back later and lay claim to a debt that was included in the bankruptcy. However, just the term "bankruptcy" itself can cast a dark shadow over what Chapter 13 does. It allows a debtor to make repayment, but at a level that can be afforded. It is not a liquidation of debt by discharge like the Chapter 7 bankruptcy.

On the same note, credit counseling makes an arrangement to repay creditors a portion of what is owed. The counseling goes a step further and educates the debtor about managing and budgeting money. You know the whole thing about teaching a person to fish and then they can feed themselves for the rest of their lives? The Chapter 13 bankruptcy is just providing a fish, not necessarily teaching a debtor how to avoid such issues in the future. The counseling reviews the credit report with the consumer to provide an understanding that will get someone back on their feet. On the downside, since the process does not utilize the legal system, there is no signature from a judge binding all parties to the terms.

So which one is better than the other? Here are some comparisons:

- With a Chapter 13 bankruptcy you would typically be dealing with an attorney who will prepare everything and make sure it is correct. What happens if they make a major mistake or file the bankruptcy incorrectly? An attorney has a professional standard to uphold and answers to their State Bar Association. A consumer has plenty of recourse to complain about a bad attorney. There is a possibility of an attorney losing his or her license if the Bar Association so chooses, although that would be extreme.

- Credit counseling is more or less a "gentlemen's agreement" to repay a portion of the debt owed over the course of a specified timeframe. What happens if one of the creditors decides to back out of the arrangement at a later point and sue for the past due amount instead? What if all creditors except one agree to the terms? If any of these things happen it could send the consumer back to square one.

- Most mortgage programs treat Chapter 13 bankruptcy and credit counseling as the same thing. Many people want to avoid the stigma of bankruptcy, but in the eyes of lenders the two things are the same. They both deal with paying off problem debts and getting back on track financially.

- Not all credit counseling agencies are alike. The most important thing to do is for a consumer to make sure the agency is accredited. Many non-profit counseling agencies are just starting out and have no idea what they're doing. In some cases they are doing more damage than good. In other cases they are just plain ripping people off. Be careful and find a credible credit counseling agency. Check with the Better Business

Bureau (www.bbb.org) before entering into any written agreements or paying out any money.

I have had several clients who have been through a Chapter 13 bankruptcy and clients who have done credit counseling. For the most part both strategies have worked well for people. From a banking standpoint it is a little bit easier to deal with a Chapter 13 bankruptcy because everything is spelled out very specifically by the court. If the credit counseling agency also updates the credit report with the consumer it can make for a cleaner transition back into reestablishing credit.

In the case of past due judgments or tax liens I would highly recommend seeking the advice of an attorney. Below is a good example of why sometimes credit counseling may not be the right choice.

Leon went through 3 years of credit counseling and paid off everything. He was ready to buy a house. I pulled his credit report and there was a judgment for over $9,000 still showing outstanding. Leon was positive the judgment was included in his debt settlement because that was his biggest concern of all. I called the credit counselor to find out what was going on. Turns out the judgment had not been included and was still owed! Leon was very disappointed. Three years of payments and none of it had knocked out that judgment!

In defense to the credit counseling industry, in Leon's case this was a counseling operation that was not accredited and would fall into the category of scam artists rather than credit counselors (they take your money and you get what you get). So if you do decide to take this route, make sure you go with an accredited company.

- You must receive 6 months of certified financial counseling prior to becoming eligible to file for bankruptcy.
- If you do not meet the "means test" for filing bankruptcy, you can still file for Chapter 13 bankruptcy.
- Chapter 13 is also known as the Wage Earner Plan. A bankruptcy trustee works with existing creditors to create a plan for the consumer to pay back debts.
- Chapter 7 bankruptcy is debt liquidation where existing debts are discharged (no longer owed).
- There are pros and cons to both Chapter 13 bankruptcy and credit counseling. Both involve making arrangements to pay off portions of the debt balance. Yet Chapter 13 is a legally binding agreement.

***

C hapter 9

Establishing Credit

"People with goals succeed because they know where they're going." - *Earl Nightingale*

Every person out there does not necessarily have a credit score, or anything contained on their credit report for that matter. While a vast majority of people do have enough credit to generate a score, a small minority do not. There are a few ways to get the ball rolling and start establishing your credit.

According to Fair Isaac, up to 50 million U.S. adults, nearly 25% of the credit eligible consumers in the U.S. have "thin files" with the major credit bureaus. Who is most likely to have a "thin file"?
- New immigrants
- Mature consumers who use mostly cash
- Young adults

***

The first step in establishing credit is to open a checking account. This sounds silly and basic, but stick with me here. A checking account gives you the ability to make payments by sending in a check when payment is due. A lender or landlord may wonder how you intend to make payment on a loan or rental if you do not have a checking account established. Obviously there are other ways to make payments such as cash, money orders, or cashier's checks. But it's not a good idea to make payments by any of those means.

When you are first getting established you have to prove yourself. Cancelled checks prove you made payment from your funds and when the lender or service provider deposited the check.

Living at home and paying rent to Mom and Dad? This is a situation that makes paying by check extremely important. If you are planning on buying a home, keep in mind that the lender will want to verify your past 12 months housing history. Paying your rent on time is essential. When a lender notices that your landlord has the same last name as you do they are going to dig deeper on verifying your rent. The only way they can do that is to request that you provide your past 12 months cancelled checks for rent. Resist the ease of handing over cash to pay for rent because this does not provide a record of payment.

This could also be true in the case of sub-leasing. If you are renting a room from someone and are not on an official lease agreement (with an apartment or property manager) you may need to back up your rental history. When you do pay by check make sure you are paying it on the first week of the month and keep the amount consistent month-to-month. If you claim you pay $500 a month and some months the check is $300 and the next month it is $800, it shows an inconsistent payment history. Keep it consistent and act as if you are paying a landlord, not a parent or friend.

The First Credit Card

It is easier for someone with no credit history to get a credit card while they are a college student than their counterparts who go directly into the work force right out of high school. Credit card companies spend a lot of money on advertising in an effort to get college students to sign-up for credit cards. Why? Number one, the credit card companies are banking on the likelihood of college students getting a good paying job once they graduate. They also know that many students receive financial assistance from their parents and will be able to pay back the borrowed money. As long as a student is careful with how they use their credit cards they can set themselves up early for a strong credit history.

Authorized User

An authorized user is a person who has been granted permission by a card holder to use a charge account. The original cardholder is solely responsible for the debt, not the authorized user. The credit card account will show up on the authorized user's credit report just like that of the original cardholder. The only difference is that the authorized user account will be indicated by an "A" coded next to the account on the credit report. A lender can look at the account and know it is just an authorized account, not an actual debt. In most cases, a lender will not count an authorized account as an open and active tradeline when making a lending decision.

Ted applies for a new mortgage. His credit is pulled by the lender and there are only two accounts listed on his credit report. The first one is a car loan that Ted opened six months ago. The second account is a credit card belonging to his mother. She added him on as an authorized user. Since Ted is not responsible for the debt, the lender won't count the authorized user account in making a lending decision. Ted's mother is fully responsible for that account. Therefore, in reality, Ted only has one open account, and that is his car loan. His car loan is only 6 months old. His lender doesn't consider this a sufficient credit history.

Most of the time an account has to be open for at least 12 months to be considered an indication that someone is likely to repay a debt. Under most circumstances we would need to have at least three accounts open for 12 months to show a sufficient history.

Also, in the above example I took the straight forward approach to how a bank views an authorized user account. The bottom line is that since the authorized user has no responsibility to pay the account, it does not count as an actual history for the authorized user. However, if the account shows a positive history then the authorized user will benefit from higher credit scores. **The purpose of being added as an authorized user is to boost the credit scores.** By having higher credit scores this will increase the chances of being approved for present and future credit. Even though it does not give the consumer an established account in their name, it can be a great benefit under the right circumstances. The best circumstance is when a computer is making the underwriting decision. Automated underwriting systems love high credit scores. It is possible an approval could be granted based on the score and the lack of established credit could be ignored.

Authorized user accounts are a two way street. We are assuming that Ted's mother has a positive history on her credit cards. What if she didn't? What if she was late last month on her payment? Ted would see the negative results on his credit report. The key to an authorized user account is that it must be positive. A negative account will bring down the overall score of the authorized user. The good news is that if you ever find yourself in this situation, you

150

may simply request to be removed from the account. As an authorized user, you can be removed as you wish.

A common question I receive about authorized user accounts is whether anything from the authorized user will show up on the cardholder's credit report. The answer is no. Unless the cardholder and authorized user co-signed for something previously, the credit reports do not merge.

Unfortunately this method of helping family members boost their scores will be short lived. In late 2007 to mid 2008 Fair Isaac Corp. will eliminate the influence of authorized user accounts in the scoring algorithm. The reason? Because people with good credit started charging money to add strangers with bad credit to their accounts. This was never the intention for the use of authorized user accounts. A few bad apples have ruined it for the rest of us.

Alternative Credit

Perhaps you don't have a friend or family member willing or able to make you an authorized user on their account. So how do you start to establish your credit?

This is where alternative credit becomes a necessity. Alternative credit would be the items we pay each month that do not show up on our credit reports. These items would include:

- Utilities
- Telephone Service (home and cellular)
- Rent
- Day Care
- Insurance Premiums
- Cable Television
- Water, Sewage, and Garbage

Anything that is paid monthly for a twelve month period could fall into the category of alternative credit. From a mortgage approval standpoint, alternative credit can and is often times a saving grace. Typically we would associate alternative credit with the government mortgage loans such as Federal Housing Administration (FHA), which requires 3% down or VA, which is for Military Veterans. When someone has no credit history it is possible to dig a little deeper to come up with something. Although it will not create a score in most cases, it is generally acceptable under certain mortgage programs.

Vinnie wants to buy a home, but he has never had credit before. He has rented for the past two years and has been employed for over two years. Vinnie is a perfect candidate for a FHA loan. He only needs three sources of alternative credit. His utilities, as long as they were paid on-time, will satisfy this requirement.

Unlike many mortgage programs FHA does not require a credit score to be approved for a mortgage. The requirement is that the borrower must have a 12 month on-time payment history for rent and preferably three other sources of alternative credit (sometimes fewer will work if there are other compensating factors such as money in the bank equaling 2 months of the new mortgage payment).

Vinnie has an electric bill, a cable bill, and a cell phone bill that he pays each month. He needs to contact each of those three services to request a payment history for the past twelve months.

Most service providers are willing to provide a payment history at no charge. The key to alternative credit is that the payments must be on-time. A lot of times we view the utilities, cable and cell phone bills as unimportant when it comes to paying them on-time. For someone with no credit history, paying everything when it is due is imperative.

If everything comes back as being paid on-time, Vinnie will have a credit history for the purpose of buying a house. If Vinnie has been late on any of these accounts he may not get approved for the loan. Once he gets his mortgage he is on his way to establishing traditional credit.

A mortgage company will typically call something late if it is paid 30 days past the due date. A couple days past the due date is not usually considered late. However, to err on the side of caution is better. Make the payment before it is due. The lender will verify the rent directly with the landlord or property manager for on-time payments.

Creating a credit history from alternative credit is a great opportunity for people who lack traditional credit. Some non-government loans allow for alternative credit also, although to a lesser extent. The traditional conventional loan is underwritten automatically by a computer. In doing this the computer relies exclusively on a credit report in order to determine whether someone is likely to repay the debt. This is where the credit scores come into play. For those who do not have credit scores or who have low credit scores, automated underwriting approvals are typically not an option. Although high income and low debt or large down payments can offset low credit scores.

The FICO® Expansion™ score is a new means for lenders to incorporate alternative credit into a credit score. This would allow lenders to make automated decisions based on the same core items that are used under FHA guidelines when a consumer does not have traditional credit.

Fair Isaac points out that the "credit-underserved" does not translate into people with bad credit. The credit-underserved are typically people who are just new to credit. These people will often times have a payment history in the service sector such as utilities, insurance, telephone, cable, internet, etc. However, these are not traditional items reported to the credit bureaus.
Government mortgage programs have allowed for these alternative sources for years, but it typically does not extend beyond that sector. Credit card companies are typically looking for a hard score that can be run through a computer to generate a decision. In dealing with alternative credit it has always been manual underwriting exclusively, which takes more time and manpower, not to mention cost.

If I take an application and run it through automated underwriting I will get a decision in less than a minute. The automated underwriting decision tells me everything I need to close the loan. Then the human underwriter is just making a check list of items that were required by the automated approval. With alternative credit the automated underwriting goes out the window, it has to be examined by a person. Now instead of an almost instant result we are talking about getting a lot of documentation and then a thorough examination of this documentation to make a credit decision. It may take an hour to come to a conclusion. For a credit card company to submit each loan application to be manually underwritten it would require a great amount of labor.

If the same information that a consumer would acquire from alternative credit sources can be reported and run through a scoring model this creates an efficient way to better serve people with little or no credit history. This opens the door for consumers to have more opportunity to become a traditional credit user.

***

Co-Signer

If you are fortunate enough to have someone co-sign for you treat the monthly payment with extreme care. You are not just establishing your own credit history; you are now controlling someone else's credit history. If you are late on your payment it will wreck what little credit you have in the short term (and haunt you for the next seven years). Beyond that, you may also cause major damage to your co-signer's credit score.

Secured Credit Cards

Secured credit cards are a good way for people to build or rebuild their credit. However, it is important to be leery of the offers made for secured credit cards. With a secured credit card you set up a savings account with a lender and borrow off of the amount you have deposited. If you deposit $500 you may only be able to borrow up to $400. You will likely have an annual fee and possibly additional costs involved in approving your application. Here are some things to watch out for:

- Make sure the issuer of the card will be reporting your account to all three of the credit bureaus. This is the main reason to get a secured credit card in the first place. If it is not reporting to the credit bureaus it is not helping your credit scores.
- If it sounds too good to be true then it likely is. Watch out for requirements of sending in an application fee. They could be targeting people just to collect an application fee only to deny the loan. Inquire about whether the application fee would be refunded if the loan is denied.
- "900" telephone numbers could be charging you just to inquire about the card.

- Interest rates could be higher than average.
- Credit repair companies that require you to sign-up for a service to get the card. Often times the card will automatically be charged for the amount of the service which could be in the $100s. Also watch out for monthly charges for services.

In a case brought against a provider of advance fee credit cards (FTC vs. Capital Choice Consumer Credit, Inc.) the judgment required the defendants to pay $36.7 million in consumer redress. A card was marketed with a $4,000 credit limit for a fee of $199.95. Consumers were led to believe that they were actually getting an unsecured credit card according to the FTC. In reality the line of credit was only for purchases made from catalogs provided by the defendants. Besides the misleading nature of what the line of credit was really for, the defendants were charging for auto club memberships and long-distance telephone cards directly through bank accounts of its customers. According to the FTC there was no authorization to charge for these additional items through bank accounts. Go to www.ftc.gov to see copies of final judgment, findings of fact, conclusions of law, and over 150 consumer related topics. There is a lot of interesting information on the FTC website.

***

- It's important to start establishing a positive credit history from the very start. And it can all begin with something as "simple" as a checking account. Paying by check can prove that you are reliable. It proves that you made payments and it can show when those payments were made.

- You can become an Authorized User on another person's account. While you are not responsible for the debt, the positive (or negative) history of that account will be reflected on your credit report and influence your credit score.
- Alternative credit, when you make timely payments, can be a great way to establish your credit. These can include utilities, cell phones, rent and so on to establish a payment history.
- If you can get someone to co-sign for a credit card or on a loan, you are both equally responsible for the debt. It is important to understand that any negative actions on your part can damage not only your credit, but the co-signer's as well.
- A secured credit card doesn't have to be a scam. It can be a good way to start building up your credit. An example would be to open an account with $500, and have $400 available credit. Keep in mind, interest rates are typically higher on these cards.

***

C hapter 10

Identity Theft

"Divide each difficulty into as many parts as necessary to resolve it." - *Rene Descartes*

It is estimated that approximately 9 million Americans are victims of identity theft each year. Scary statistic. And it usually starts at home.

Whether it is a relative or a roommate, the root of the crime does not always go beyond the front door of your home. When I review credit reports with clients it is not uncommon for people to tell me that various accounts do not belong to them. I would say that 50% of the time when someone states that they were a victim of ID theft the culprit is someone they know. This creates a problem especially when it is a relative because the victim does not want to involve the police. As a lender, if we are going to argue a negative account as being the result of ID theft we need evidence. The best evidence is a police report. When I ask for a police report to back up our claim, people tell me they are not willing to involve the police since it was a relative.

Thelma is the epitome of a loving grandmother. When she came to me, we found numerous past due accounts in her name. Those accounts had actually been opened by

158

Thelma's grandchild. Thelma refused to involve the police. She was actually willing to pay off the bad debts! She wanted to clear up her credit without getting her grandchild in trouble with the law.

Most Common Sources of Identity Theft:
28.8% Lost or stolen wallet, checkbook or credit card
11.6% Internet
11.4% Someone known
 8.7% Offline transaction
 8.7% Employee
 8.0% Mail
 2.6% Garbage

***

Interview with an Identity Theft Detective

To get a true feel for identity theft you need to talk to someone who deals with it everyday. I interviewed a detective who spent four years investigating identity theft related crimes. Talk about an interesting conversation!

Almost 100% of the time these ID crimes are connected to drugs, most commonly methamphetamines. When the police bust a meth lab it is not uncommon to discover a room filled with of boxes of mail. People on meth tend to not sleep for days and this gives them plenty of time to steal mail and then go through it. Not to mention going through dumpsters looking for sensitive information.

Catching mail thieves will sometimes lead back to the meth lab for a larger scale bust. Since stealing mail is a Federal crime, law enforcement can leverage the scale of the crime to get more information out of the criminal. The mail thief is at the bottom of the totem pole when it comes to identity theft, but they are a good source of information leading to the arrest of the ring leader.

Identity thieves typically work in specialized areas. The guy who steals mail teams up with someone who knows how to make fake identification. From there they team up with someone who can make bogus checks. A name taken off of a bank account can then be made into an ID with the criminal's face. Making a check with the account numbers from the bank statement then allows the thief to go out and write checks against an existing account. It may take weeks before the victim catches on to what is happening. A lot of times the thieves will make purchases at a store and then go to a different location to return the merchandise for cash.

Typically ID thieves are opportunists who are repeat offenders. Some of them believe identity theft is a victimless crime because they think the bank incurs the loss, not the consumer. They look for the easiest way to steal a buck. One ID thief told the detective, "I am better off taking an ID for $30,000 than robbing a bank for $5,000 and facing an automatic 10 years." It can be hard to identify these people because the crime may not be discovered for a stretch of time. A store camera may recycle every couple weeks. By the time the crime is discovered the tapes could have been erased. Some stores have digital cameras that can record months of footage. The best thing to do is report these crimes as soon as they are discovered to have a better chance of identifying the culprit.

Identifying the suspects even when there is a photo can be challenging. If it is not someone the detectives are familiar with, they only have a face, no name or any other way to find the person. A lot of times the photo will be forwarded to other agencies and jurisdictions to see if it is someone they recognize. Ultimately the photo may end up in the jail with the hopes that the suspect will be picked up on other charges at some point and the jailers will recognize the suspect.

Once a suspect is caught, the entire ring may soon come crashing down. The guy writing the checks may turn in the person making the checks. In return, the check maker rats out the person who provided the names.

In some cases the fraud did not stem from mail theft, but from database theft. This leads to other possible criminal charges because now there may be a business that had its client information compromised. The original suspect may lead back to a computer tech that took client information from a business. This is not uncommon, especially when the detectives interview victims and find a common thread.

Imagine this scenario: *You visit a medical office once. You provide your name, your date of birth and your social security number so the visit can be paid for by your insurance company. A year later you receive a letter stating that your personal information may have been compromised. Apparently, many recent victims of identity fraud in the area have a common link. They had all visited this particular medical office. How did your information and the information of fellow patients get into the hands of ID thieves? The computer tech for the business was stealing the information off the company computers and selling the information in exchange for drugs.*

Scary stuff. And it happens more often than we'd like to think.

The most commonly misused social security number of all time was 078-05-1120. In 1938 a wallet maker used a sample social security card to show how the card could fit into the wallet. A company executive thought it would be clever to use the actual social security number of his secretary, Mrs. Hilda Schrader Whitcher. The sample was inserted in each wallet the company manufactured. The wallet was sold by department stores all over the United States.

Many purchasers of the wallet decided to use the social security number on the sample card as their own. By 1943, 5,755 people were using the social security number. Mrs. Whitcher was assigned a new number and her original number was voided. Overall 40,000 people used 078-05-1120 as their social security number, as recently as 1977.

***

Identity Theft Online

Technology has opened the flood gates to identity thieves. Knowing what to watch for can prevent you from being a victim. Avoid clicking on pop-up advertisements, you could inadvertently download spyware. Spyware gathers information without your knowledge. It could provide access to your login and password for sensitive website accounts allowing a criminal to get into your accounts.

Phishing is another cyber-crime to watch out for. Phishing is when someone creates a fake website designed to look like it belongs to a major company. Typically it would be a situation where login and password or credit card information could be entered and stolen to be used fraudulently. Sites that sell items can be a target since a credit card number could be entered by a consumer thinking they are on the real website. Then the credit card number is used to make unauthorized purchases. Most people fall victim to this by responding to a spam email that has a link to the fake website. Typically the email message will say that information needs to be updated or the account will be terminated. Phishing is on the rise according to the Anti-Phishing Working Group. For more information go to www.antiphishing.org.

Do you buy things online using your debit card? Are you using the four-digit pin from your debit card as a password for other logins? If so, you may be setting yourself up for identity theft.

Lauren had her debit card number and pin code stolen while shopping online. She was at work and what she did not know was that someone had tapped into her company's internet. They were able to see her online movements. Lauren logged into a store website and made her purchase with her debit card. Her password for the store login? Her four digit pin. Even though the password was blocked out on the screen, the criminal was able to figure it out. When Lauren checked out of the online store, her debit card number was right there on the screen for the criminal to easily copy down. A couple days later $500 was mysteriously withdrawn from an ATM from both Lauren's checking and savings accounts. The thief rolled the dice that the password Lauren used on the website and her pin would be the exact same. Needless to say, the ATM camera caught a person with their face covered.

How could a thief possibly get cash out of an ATM without the actual debit card? That magnetic strip on the back of your debit card contains your account number. An ATM (or any card machine) is able to read the magnetic strip and with the password, gain access to the account. Think about the last time you stayed at a hotel…did you get a key? Most likely you were given a magnetic card programmed with the combination to open your room door. A criminal with one of these magnetic card programming machines can simply program in the account number and create a bank card. Don't make things easy for the bad guys. Make sure you do not use your pin number as a password for other things.

eBay has had some recent scams striking its customers. The first one is the "Second Chance Offer" you may receive if you are the second highest bidder on an auction. Some internet thieves are watching high dollar auctions and contacting the second highest bidder after the auction. They pose as the seller and make their fake email look exactly like the real "Second Chance Offer" email. When the person agrees to buy the item they are steered toward paying through Western Union (cash) instead of through the eBay PayPal site. If you are ever asked to pay through Western Union it is probably a scam. Always respond to all correspondence through the eBay website itself, and make sure the message you received via email is in your Message Center. If not, it is likely a fraud.

Another eBay scam is receiving a fake email message from an eBay member asking if you are willing to be paid by PayPal (usually targeting people who have sold on EBay recently). I personally received one of these and it almost tricked me. Of course I would be "willing" to accept PayPal. My auctions clearly state that PayPal is the preferred method of payment. I smelled a rat. But boy did that email look real! The email had a real-looking icon to log into eBay. If I had logged in I would have been taken to the internet thief's website (set up to look like eBay). Thinking I was in eBay I would have logged in and now the thief would have my password. Armed with this they might be able to access my PayPal account and steal my money (eBay and PayPal passwords should be different as a precaution). The first thing to realize is that anything sent to you via email by eBay can be found inside the eBay website in your Message Center. I went into eBay and sure enough there was no message from the particular member I received the email from. I looked up the member and contacted them through eBay and they had not sent me anything regarding PayPal. The internet thief was able to see all the information they needed to try to trick me by just going to the eBay member profile. I forwarded the email to eBay Security and it was confirmed to be a fake.

Make sure you type in the correct website address for any sites that require you to have a login and password you would not want anyone else to know. There are numerous websites out there that are misspellings of specific website addresses hoping to lure people onto the wrong site. Sometimes it is just a marketing ploy, but on occasion it is a criminal hoping to gain sensitive information.

Compromised Data

We do all we can personally to reduce identity theft, but our information is out there in databases and computer systems that we have no control over. I did an unscientific study of the major breaches of data in 2005. This is based only on organizations that made notice of the security breach. Here are the number of information breaches by business category:

Colleges/Universities	55
Banks/Financial Services	17
Other Corporations	17
Government Agencies	13
Hospital/Medical	5
Retailer	4
Non-profit	2

Not all breaches are included as some may have only been reported on a local scale or were very minor. For example, a breach at a small doctor's office isn't likely to make the news.

Over 420,000,000 Social Security numbers have been issued since 1936. Social Security numbers are not reissued once a holder is deceased. About 5.5 million new numbers are issued each year. Under the current numbering system there are enough combinations to go generations into the future without a change to the number of digits.

***

If you are a victim of a security breach you will most likely be notified by mail as to the nature of the information that was stolen. The best thing to do is check your credit report for inquiries on your report since the date of the breach. You can add a fraud alert to your credit report to let lenders know your identity may have been compromised. An initial fraud alert only lasts for 90 days. A more extensive alert may be granted by writing the credit bureaus directly and including a copy of a police report. In some cases you may be able to get a fraud alert for up to seven years. Check your credit every few months to watch for unknown accounts and most importantly to see the inquiries made on your credit report.

The list of inquiries is your best indicator as to whether someone has recently attempted to open credit in your name. If a thief is able to establish credit in your name it may take two to three months before the account will appear on your report. An inquiry will appear immediately and will identify who looked at the credit and when. Most reports will list the inquiries for the past 90 days; that is why you would want to check your report at least every three months if you suspect the possibility of fraud.

Rights for Identity Theft Victims

You have the right to request the credit bureaus place fraud alerts on your credit report. Potential creditors will then be aware that your information has been exposed and that the applicant may not be you. Greater care to fully identify the applicant is what usually results from the fraud alert. A fraud alert will stay on the credit report for 90 days. If you have filed a police report an extended alert may be put in place. This could be a report filed with local, state, or federal law enforcement. You will need to provide a copy of the report to the credit bureaus.

You have the right to copies of your credit report. The initial fraud alert entitles you to a single copy of your report from each of the three credit bureaus in a 12 month period. An extended alert will allow you to obtain two free reports in a 12 month period.

You have the right to copies of documents relating to the fraudulent transactions or accounts opened using your information. Applications and other business records must be provided by the creditor involved in the incident if you make a request in writing. If the business refuses to make the documents available, you should contact the Federal Trade Commission to register a complaint. There are some circumstances where a business may not have to provide the requested information. The FTC can inform you based on your situation whether the business is breaking any laws.

You may request the credit bureaus to block information from your file that was the result of identity theft. Follow the bureaus' instructions for the proper documentation that will be required. You may also request the business involved in the incident to not report information to the credit bureaus if it is connected to identity theft.

Preventing Identity Theft

- Don't give out personal information on the phone, through the mail or over the Internet unless you've initiated the contact.
- Do not carry your social security card with you. It is best to put it in a safe deposit box and only take it out when you need it.
- Shred everything. Make sure you use a confetti-cut machine. The straight-cut shredders make a "meth head puzzle," which can be taped back together. Yes, people on meth are rummaging through dumpsters at night, and yes, they spend the rest of the night taping things back together. I personally use a Fellowes brand shredder. I also recommend shredding non-sensitive documents to mix more paper in with your sensitive documents.
- Check your mail everyday, even if you have a locked mailbox. Criminals find ways to steal master keys and open up the entire box.
- Put a hold on your mail delivery when going on vacation.
- Only put mail in the blue Post Office boxes or another secure mailbox. Never put outgoing mail in an unsecured mailbox.
- Check your bank accounts frequently to look for activities you did not initiate.
- Call 1-888-5-OPTOUT (1-888-567- 8688). You will be asked for your Social Security number in

order for the credit bureaus to identify your file so that they can remove you from their lists.

- Do not carry all of your credit cards, only the ones you need or use.
- Give your social security number out only when absolutely necessary.
- Pay attention that your bills are arriving when expected. If statements are not arriving, it could be an indication that someone changed your mailing address to receive your information.
- Be aware of phony offers. Claims of sweepstakes and other "bait" could be a ploy to get your information.
- Try to pick up your new checks at the bank rather than having them mailed to you.

Procedures If You Are Victim

- Move quickly to prevent any further misuse of your information.
- Call every credit card company you have an account with to let them know your situation.
- Call your bank to alert them to the circumstances whether it was your bank statements, debit card or checks that may have been compromised.
- Every call you make should be followed up in writing. Sending certified letters provides you with documentation that your requests for action were made.
- File a police report and get a copy for your records. Typically you need to file with the jurisdiction the crime occurred in. In the case of mail theft, contact a postal inspector. If the local police will not file a report, try the county sheriff. If that does not work go to the state police, then the FBI. The main thing is to keep trying until you get a report filed.

- Follow-up with the fraud departments of any institution involved in the theft. Whether it is your credit card company or the store in which the fraud took place.
- Request to file affidavits with any entity that had a loss in the theft. This is your statement of non-involvement in the crime. Keep copies for your records.
- For all lost identity cards contact the issuing agency or office.
- If you feel you are not getting results move up the chain of command. It may be necessary to contact your State Attorney General's Office or Federal agencies such as the Federal Trade Commission, Federal Deposit Insurance Corporation, Federal Reserve, or Office of the Comptroller of the Currency. Keep copies of all complaints or correspondence.

- Prevent ID theft – read the bullet points on the previous pages.
- ID theft may hit close to home. Make sure family members and friends do not have access to your sensitive information.
- Keep your eye on your credit reports. See a bunch of inquiries? Could be an ID thief has your personal information and is trying to obtain credit in your name.
- Do you think you have been the recent victim of ID theft? Read the bullet points on the previous pages on procedures to follow.
- Protect yourself online. Never follow links from an email. Avoid pop-ups and download the latest firewalls and privacy software.

- Vary your pin numbers and passwords. Don't make it easy for a thief to figure out a PIN and access your accounts.

***

Chapter 11

Mortgages and Credit

There is a lot of information out there comparing mortgage interest rates across different levels of credit scores. Comparisons can be somewhat deceptive because there are so many variables that go into a mortgage approval, as well as the varying programs on the market. Someone with a 720 credit score could end up with the same interest rate as someone with a score of 580 depending on the overall picture (i.e. FHA).

Conventional mortgages are the bulk of the mortgages being done in the market and are often the benchmark for comparing interest rates. Yet, there are government loans such as FHA that offer comparable rates. FHA will give the same rate to someone with no credit score at all versus someone with a 720 credit score. On a conventional loan the rate will usually go up by .375 when someone is under a 620 credit score. FHA mortgages have no rate increase based on credit score, although there is typically a cutoff for approval if someone is under a 550 credit score (it would be better to have no score at all).

Automated underwriting has leveled the playing field for consumers in a sense. Someone with a 720 credit score, but little money in the bank would likely have the same approval as someone with a 650 credit score, but a lot of money in a retirement account. The automated underwriting weighs all the variables such as credit scores, time since last delinquency, debt-to-income ratios, length of time with current job, down payment, liquid assets (checking, savings, retirement, CD's, money markets, etc.), in some cases the type of property, and makes a decision based on all of this information. High credit scores always get kudos with automated underwriting. Great credit can outweigh a lack of assets and income a lot of times.

Conventional Mortgage

This is the most common mortgage program consumers use. Down payment ranges from zero to 20% or more. A common down payment would be 5% of the sales price. Anything less will usually result in a slightly higher rate. Income and assets need to be fully verified in most cases. However, for people with high credit scores (720+) they could get an approval that does not require documentation of income through pay stubs and W2's, just a verbal verification of employment. Conventional loans are almost always underwritten automatically, although a few conventional programs allow for manual underwriting.

Government Mortgage

This usually refers to FHA, VA, or USDA. Rural Housing and must be for primary residences. FHA mortgages require 3% down, whereas VA and USDA are zero down loans. VA is only available to Military Veterans, while the USDA mortgage is for people residing in areas classified as rural populations. Government loans are usually run through automated underwriting initially, but if the computer does not like it, that file will go to a human for underwriting (manual underwriting). Government loans have different guidelines for credit than conventional loans. A conventional loan looks strongly at the score and payment history for the past two years. The government loans do not look at the scores as much. The biggest factor is the payment history in the past twelve months. For someone who has been on-time for the past twelve months and does not have any past due collections a government mortgage is a good option.

Stated Income

This is a loan designed for people who cannot document their income. Self employed individuals use this type of loan most often, but so do people who earn a lot of cash tips such as bartenders, hair stylists, massage therapists, servers, entertainers, etc. With a stated income loan the lender will verify the length of time in the line of work, but not the actual amount of income. Two years in the same line of work is a requirement. Self employed borrowers have to prove two years of self employment through verification by an accountant, tax preparer, or business license. Stated income loans come at a higher interest rate than a full documentation conventional loan. Interest rates for stated income loans are influenced by two major factors: credit scores and down payment. The higher the credit scores, the lower the rate. More down payment, the lower the rate. Since we do not have documentation of actual income these other two factors are monumental to obtain an approval. It's possible to do a zero down stated income; in fact someone could do this down to a 640 credit score (although requirements do change periodically). This is where we see a big difference in interest rates between levels of credit score. A borrower with a 720 is likely to get a rate 2% to 3% better than someone with a 640 credit score. The terms are a lot worse for the borrower with a 640 credit score as they would likely be offered a 2-year adjustable mortgage, as opposed to the 30-year fixed term the 720 borrower could get for less interest. The borrower with a 640 could get a 30-year fixed interest rate if they really wanted it, but then it might be an increase of 4% -

5% over what the borrower with a 720 would get. Why so high? Keep in mind that the zero down stated income loan is probably the most risky mortgage a lender can make. You have a borrower who cannot document income and who has no money being put toward the property. Talk about risk! Especially if you have a borrower who may have had problems managing their credit in the past. This is a good example of why a good credit score is so important. Managing our debts can pay dividends later when we want something, such as a house.

Stated Income / Stated Asset

This is the same as stated income, except the twist is now we are stating the assets. There is no verification of the balances of bank accounts. Now we can only base an approval on credit scores and down payment. This is a step up in risk, but a minor one. The rates on these types of loans will not be much higher than the plain stated income, maybe .125 to .250 higher. Stating the assets may be necessary if the down payment is cash under the mattress, or a gift from a friend or a relative. Any time there is no direct paper trail for large amounts of money it could be a problem. If someone has a two month average balance of $2,000 in their bank account and then before they apply for a loan there is all of a sudden $30,000 in the account we would need to verify where the extra $28,000 came from. There are plenty of acceptable explanations, as long as there is some sort of paper trail for where the money came from. In a case where there is no acceptable explanation or no way to document where the money came from, that is when we turn to stated assets.

No Doc (No Documentation)

This type of mortgage requires no income verification, employment verification, or asset verification. The only documentation is the credit report and the previous housing history. The credit scores are extremely important on no doc loans and the underwriter will go through the credit report with a fine tooth comb. A late payment from 6 years ago will probably require a written explanation. This is a fairly straightforward loan, although first time homebuyers could have trouble qualifying if their rent payment is not close to the new mortgage payment. There are various no doc programs and they all have different requirements. This is a popular loan for people who just sold a business, who are retired, who are in between jobs, people who have been self employed less than two years, or live off investments exclusively.

Second Mortgage / Home Equity Line of Credit (HELOC)

This deals with pulling cash out of equity and is a popular means to do things to increase the value of your home or to make some other major purchase. Second mortgages look at the credit scores to determine how much equity a borrower may tap. Someone with a 720 could probably pull out cash equaling 100% of the value of their home. While someone with a 660 might only be able to access 90% or less. The lower the credit score the less available equity for cash.

Second Home Loan

Second homes must be at least 50 miles from your primary residence. If it is not 50 miles away it will likely have to go as an investment property. The down payments range from zero to as much as you want to put down. Someone buying a second home with a conventional loan probably will not notice a difference in the rate from what a primary residence would be, as long as they were doing a full documentation on the income.

176

I was once asked while speaking at Arizona State University, "What is the most important thing an investor should focus on for acquiring numerous rental properties?" The answer: CREDIT. Credit scores are the key to investment loans. Employment, assets, and down payment amount are certainly also major factors to an approval, but credit makes it happen. The investors that I typically deal with plan to acquire more than one investment property. We sit down and talk about the things in this book, how does one achieve optimum credit scores? How do we protect our credit? The answers to these questions are necessary because we may need to strengthen the credit position before we can get into a lifetime of real estate investing. Now we are talking not only about the impact of credit on interest rates but also about lost money-making opportunities. All the time I get people who have strong income, have money in the bank and are ready to dive into real estate investing. A lot of times they took their credit for granted, a late payment here and there, a collection or two. If you take care of business and go out of your way to have great credit you will put yourself in a superior position when it comes to borrowing money. Especially when it comes to borrowing money to make money such as real estate investing.

***

- The bottom line: higher credit scores mean more options and better interest rates.

***

Appendix A: Legislation

"Laws too gentle are seldom obeyed; too severe, seldom executed." - *Benjamin Franklin*

Brace yourself. Some of you may find this tedious legal mumbo-jumbo just a waste of space. If that's you, then go ahead and skip the section. There are other readers (really, there are!) that like to know about the nitty-gritty legal stuff that concerns credit issues. The Acts are in alphabetical order, not chronological.

Community Reinvestment Act
In 1977, Congress enacted the Community Reinvestment Act (CRA) to require banks, thrifts, and other lenders to make capital available in low- and moderate-income urban neighborhoods, thereby boosting the nation's efforts to stabilize these declining areas.

Consumer Credit Protection Act of 1968
This Federal legislation established rules for the disclosure of the terms of a loan to protect borrowers. In turn, this piece of legislation launched the Truth-in-Lending Act. This was the first time that creditors were required to state the cost of borrowing in a universal language so that consumers could figure out the true cost of borrowing. This allows consumers to compare offers and make a decision that is best for them.

Disposal Rule
On June 1st, 2005 a new rule took effect requiring the proper disposal of consumer information. It was set forth to prevent sensitive financial and personal information from getting into the hands of criminals. The new rule expanded a former rule on information disposal to include <u>any</u>

industry disposing of data that would be considered "consumer information."

"Consumer information" is typically defined as information stemming from a consumer report or a variation of such information. Typically any information gained from a third-party would fall into the category of "consumer information" and would therefore fall under the Disposal Rule. When a business collects information on its own directly from a consumer this is not considered "consumer information" and is not subject to the Disposal Rule. However, businesses should adhere to the philosophy that all sensitive information that could lead to identity theft will fall into the Disposal Rule.

The Disposal Rule includes both paperwork and electronic data on computers. There is no specific set of rules regarding what constitutes disposal. The FTC has published this statement, "The FTC realizes there are few foolproof methods of records destruction and that entities covered by the rule must consider their own unique circumstances when determining how to best comply with the rule." Non-compliance could result in a $2,500 penalty per violation and is open to private lawsuits by consumers.

***

Electronic Funds Transfer Act and Fair Credit Billing Act

Established procedures for resolving mistakes on credit billing and electronic fund transfer account statements, including:

- charges or electronic fund transfers that you – or anyone you have authorized to use your account – have not made;

- charges or electronic fund transfers that are incorrectly identified or show the wrong date or amount;
- math errors;
- failure to post payments, credits, or electronic fund transfers properly;
- failure to send bills to your current address – provided the creditor receives your change of address, in writing, at least 20 days before the billing period ends;
- charges or electronic fund transfers for which you ask for an explanation or written proof of purchase along with a claimed error or request for clarification.

Equal Credit Opportunity Act

Prohibits a creditor from discriminating against a consumer on the basis of age, sex, marital status, reliance on income from public assistance, race, color, religion, or national origin.

Fair and Accurate Credit Transactions Act of 2003 (FACTA)

Under this Act consumers may now dispute inaccurate information directly with the creditor that has reported the information originally. Previously the law only required the credit bureaus to investigate claims of inaccurate information. Creditors may not report the negative information in question while the investigation is pending. Although if the investigation determines the information is correct, it will be reported again.

Fair Credit and Charge Card Disclosure Act of 1988

Amended the Truth in Lending Act to require new disclosures of information in connection with credit card and charge card account applications and solicitations. All solicitations must disclose credit card fees, APR, grace period and balance calculation method.

Fair Credit Reporting Act

The main purpose is to ensure that consumer information is accurate and confidential. The design is to promote accuracy, fairness, and privacy of information in the files of every consumer reporting agency.

Fair Debt Collection Practices Act

Collectors are prevented from certain abusive techniques in an attempt to collect a debt. This applies to personal, family, and household debts. And it includes money you owe for the purchase of a car, for medical care, or for charge accounts. The FDCPA prohibits debt collectors from engaging in unfair, deceptive, or abusive practices while collecting these debts. Under the Fair Debt Collection Practices Act:

- Debt collectors may contact you only between 8 a.m. and 9 p.m.
- Debt collectors may not contact you at work if they know your employer disapproves.
- Debt collectors may not harass, oppress, or abuse you.
- Debt collectors may not lie when collecting debts, such as falsely implying that you have committed a crime.
- Debt collectors must identify themselves to you on the phone.
- Debt collectors must stop contacting you if you ask them to do so in writing.

The Identity Theft and Assumption Deterrence Act of 1998

Amends the Federal Criminal Code to make it unlawful for anyone to knowingly transfer or use, without lawful authority, a means of identification of another person with the intent to commit, or to aid or abet, any unlawful activity that constitutes a violation of Federal law, or that constitutes a felony under any applicable State or local law.

Real Estate Settlement Procedures Act (RESPA)
This law protects consumers from abuses during the residential real estate purchase and loan process and enables them to be better informed shoppers by requiring disclosure of costs of settlement services.

Truth in Lending Act (TILA)
Requires creditors to provide a consumer with accurate and complete credit costs and terms. This is measured by the Annual Percentage Rate (APR), which creates an apples for apples approach to comparing loan offers. It also established requirements for advertisers to disclose credit terms.

Appendix B: Credit Test

Here are a series of questions to test your credit IQ:

1. What government entity enforces consumer rights pertaining to credit?
   a. The Better Business Bureau (BBB)
   b. The Federal Communications Commission (FCC)
   c. The Federal Trade Commission (FTC)
   d. Housing and Urban Development (HUD)
2. Which is the best score below in terms of credit scores?
   a. 499
   b. 699
   c. 800
   d. 100
3. Which of these could be affected by your credit?
   a. Employment
   b. Loan approval
   c. Insurance premium
   d. All of the above
4. How long does a late payment stay on your credit report?
   a. Until it is brought current
   b. Until you close the account
   c. Until seven years has passed
   d. Until you go 12 months with on-time payments
5. What happens if a lender does not report your account to the credit bureaus?
   a. They can be fined by the FTC
   b. They can be forced by the credit bureaus
   c. They could lose their banking license
   d. They are not required by law to report

6. How much does it cost you for the credit bureaus to investigate your dispute?
    a. Nothing, it is free
    b. $14.95 per credit bureau
    c. $9.99 for all three credit bureaus
    d. It varies depending on how many accounts need to be disputed
7. Who is the creator of the current credit scoring model?
    a. The Federal Trade Commission
    b. The Federal Reserve
    c. The Federal Depository Insurance Corporation (FDIC)
    d. Fair Isaac Corporation
8. If your checking account balance is under $100, what will happen to your credit scores?
    a. The scores will decline
    b. Nothing as long as the balance exceeds $50
    c. Nothing, checking accounts are not part of the scoring model
    d. Nothing, that is the balance the score looks for
9. Which of these is not on your credit report?
    a. Social Security number
    b. Available credit limits
    c. Current balances on debts
    d. Current balances on savings accounts
10. Which of the following could report information on you to the credit bureaus?
    a. Courts / County Recorder
    b. Federal Trade Commission
    c. Your employer
    d. State Bar Association

11. Which process discharges all debt included in the procedure?
    a. Chapter 13 bankruptcy
    b. Credit Counseling
    c. Chapter 7 bankruptcy
    d. Disputing with the credit bureaus
12. Which mortgage program does not require a credit score?
    a. Stated income
    b. No documentation
    c. FHA
    d. Second mortgage
13. Which of the following would be a source of alternative credit?
    a. Utilities
    b. Car insurance
    c. Cellular phone
    d. All of the above
14. Which factors influence your credit score?
    a. Paying on-time
    b. Keeping your revolving balances low
    c. A longer account history
    d. All of the above
15. The better your credit score, the more likely you are to get the best terms on a loan.
    a. True
    b. False
16. You are allowed to get a free copy of your credit report for any reason as many times throughout the year as necessary.
    a. True
    b. False
17. A divorce decree will not protect your credit.
    a. True
    b. False

18. Closing all of your credit card accounts could hurt your credit scores in the future.
    a. True
    b. False
19. Paying your balance on a credit card in full each month will ensure your scores are always at the highest possible.
    a. True
    b. False
20. When you co-sign with someone you have equal responsibility for the debt being paid.
    a. True
    b. False

Answers:

1. C   The Federal Trade Commission oversees the laws pertaining to our nation's credit.

2. C   The higher the credit score the better.

3. D   Credit affects more just our loan approvals. Insurance premiums and employment opportunities can also be weighed by our credit profile.

4. C   Only the passage of time will remedy a late payment, unless you can successfully dispute the accuracy of a late payment.

5. D   Reporting to the credit bureaus is purely voluntary and is not required. Creditors report by choice, and the majority will. Smaller organizations may not report due to organizational constraints. If your creditor is not reporting it is worth requesting them to do so.

6. A   There is no cost to investigate your dispute.

7. D   Fair Isaac Corporation is the creator of the FICO® score, the most commonly used scoring model.

8. C   Checking account balances do not factor into the credit scoring model, nor would the balances appear on the credit report.

9. D   The credit report does not contain depository balances.

10. A   Judgments and tax liens are reported to the credit bureaus by courts and recording offices.

11. C   Chapter 7 bankruptcy discharges debt that does not have to be repaid.

12. C   FHA mortgages do not require a credit score unlike the majority of mortgage programs.

13. D   Alternative sources of credit can be anything in your name that has been paid on-time on a monthly basis. It is typically something that would not be reported on a credit report.

14. D The credit scores consider more than just making payments on-time. Revolving balances and account age are major factors in the credit scores.

15. A This is true because credit scores reflect our likelihood to repay money.

16. B There are certain circumstances in which a person can receive a free copy of their credit report. Everyone is entitled to a free copy of their credit report once a year from each of the three major credit bureaus. People who have been a victim of identity theft, have disputed an error, have been denied based on information contained in their credit report, are on public assistance, or are unemployed and seeking employment may also receive a free copy of their credit report at the time of the circumstances.

17. A A divorce decree simply assigns responsibility of debt to a party in the proceedings. It does not protect credit from late payments made by the assigned party if the account is held jointly.

18. A Closing credit card accounts is not good for credit scores. The reason is that the length of time an account has been open is a factor in the scoring model (15% of the equation). Total credit utilization of revolving accounts (credit cards) has an impact on the credit scores. Closing a credit card reduces the total amount of available credit and can result in a decline of credit scores.

19. B Paying off a balance in full each month is a good idea. However, it does not ensure the credit scores will always be at the highest possible point. When a credit report is ordered it is a snapshot of that moment in time. If a credit card happens to be at the limit available, the credit scores will not be as high as they could be. Even for someone who pays off a credit card in full each month it is still necessary to watch that the balance does not get above 50% of

the available limit. Maintaining where our balances are on credit cards is almost as important as paying our bills on-time.

20. A   When someone co-signs for a loan it is a joint account and there is equal responsibility for both parties to make sure payments are made on-time. For someone with good credit the biggest risk they may have is co-signing with a person who does not make the payment on-time. Co-signing with another person requires much consideration and should be viewed from the standpoint of whether you could handle the payment if the other person could not.

Appendix C: Frequently Asked Questions

Does my credit report list if I have EVER filed bankruptcy? Only for 10 years from the discharge date.

What is binding mandatory arbitration?
When a company requires a customer to agree to submit all possible disputes to arbitration prior to completing a transaction with the company. In binding mandatory arbitration a customer is waiving the right to sue, participate in a class action lawsuit, or appeal. This is also known as Dispute Resolution Mechanism, and is often found in the fine print of a contract. In some cases there is a separate form a customer would be required to sign outside of a contract.

What is the final straw if I am not having any luck disputing inaccurate information on my credit report?
The final step would be to file a complaint with the FTC since this is the government entity that enforces the Fair Credit Reporting Act. It is also possible to sue the creditor and the credit bureau reporting the information. If you go to this step you will need good evidence backing your claim. You should probably consult a consumer credit attorney before taking legal action. It may cost money, but at least you will know if you have a reasonable case.

My credit card company notified me that my interest rate is increasing. Why do they do that?
There could be several reasons:
- You were late on your payment
- You went over your available credit limit
- You were late on a different account with a different lender. (In the agreement you signed to receive your credit card it could have a provision regarding an

increase in your rate if you become delinquent on any account under your name).

Is there a recommended number of credit cards a person should have?

There really is not a specific number. However, I would recommend at least three for the long run. Since we want our cards to reach the seven year mark, to really boost our scores we want to have enough "cushion" so that if one is closed for some reason the remaining cards will still provide an adequate history. Personally I have 10+ open and active credit cards. Two I use and pay off each month (although I never go above 50% of the available balance at any point in the month). The rest I use maybe annually to have enough activity to keep them open. My cards are all in an age range of 13 -15 years old, so I have a good amount of history there that I would not want to lose. Since most of my cards are rarely used it doesn't hurt my score to have that much available credit. Many people say that having a lot of available credit is a bad thing, and it can be, if you use all of it. For those who have it available and rarely use it there is nothing to be all that concerned about.

One of my clients, Jose, has 8 credit cards open and active. All over 7 years with nothing else, no car payment, no student loans, no mortgage, just credit cards. His combined available limit is $80,000, but his balances are $0. Jose's middle credit score is 799. Not too shabby.

Does a 401(k) loan appear on the credit report? No

What is the VantageScore$_{sm}$?

VantageScore was announced in March 2006 by the three major credit bureaus as an easy to understand formula to credit scoring. The collaboration by the three bureaus is known as VantageScore Solutions, LLC. The advantage being touted is consistency in scoring across the three credit bureaus. The scoring ranges would be two-tiered:

VantageScore range: 500-990

901 - 990 = A
801 - 900 = B
701 -800 = C
601 - 700 = D
501 - 600 = F

This does not appear to accomplish the "easy to understand" angle VantageScore claims. In fact, to achieve true consistency in credit scoring the three bureaus would have to report the same identical information. Since this is not the case it does not appear that the VantageScore model offers anything beneficial for consumers or lenders.

This is not the first time a credit scoring model has been rolled out to compete with the FICO® model, nor will it be the last. The problem with copycat scoring models is the new models do not have the depth of history the FICO® model has. On the surface one might think we are only talking about credit scores and how these scores might differ from one model to another. Not quite.

Fannie Mae and Freddie Mac are the two congressionally chartered corporations that oversee the mortgage world. The two entities set precedence in regards to mortgage underwriting guidelines. Currently they have only approved FICO® scores to be used in the automated underwriting systems used for approving mortgages. It would be a large undertaking to change this over to a new and unproven scoring model. Institutional investors rely on the underwriting guidelines to provide secure investments in the mortgage backed securities arena. Nomura Securities

International said in a March 2006 report, "In our opinion, VantageScore faces a tough, uphill fight."

An April 2006 administrative announcement by the USDA Rural Development stated, "Most automated underwriting systems are built to use FICO® scores, and reconfiguring them will take time and money. Industry participants, including the Federal Housing Administration (FHA), Veteran Affairs (VA), Fannie Mae, and Freddie Mac, do not accept VantageScore at this time." At this point it does not appear people will be gathering around the water cooler to compare their VantageScore.

How long does it take for credit scores to go up?
Credit scores can change daily, depending on when information on the credit report changes. For someone with low credit scores, say 520, it will take positive information being reported or more time since the negative information was first reported to see the scores increase. If the reason the scores are low is because of frequent late payments, just the act of paying on-time will increase the scores. When someone is late in the current month and that is the only negative thing on the credit report, it will take about a year to see a significant increase in the scores. For example, if you have a 650 credit score and have two late payments that drop your score down to 550, a year from the late dates the scores might be back to 650 if nothing else negative occurred. The thing to remember is the scoring model considers so many things that a combination of negative items can keep the scores lower longer.

Late payments combined with past due collections and high credit card balances will make it more difficult for the credit scores to go up. The biggest reason I see scores stay low is because there is nothing positive going into the credit report. For someone with no active accounts (loans being paid on currently) and only collections, there is

193

nothing that will make the scores go up except the passage of time from the dates the collections were reported. Paying off the collections ASAP would most likely be the greatest benefit for this scenario. Once the collections are paid make sure they are corrected on the credit report. Keep in mind the scores could suffer a slight decline in the short term as once the collections are reported as being paid in full the dates will be reported more recently. However, for someone in the low 500 range this is not a big deal since the goal is to ultimately make the scores higher. You have to have a starting point and in this scenario, paying off the collections would be the starting point.

If negative items occurred years ago there will be a gradual increase in the scores as the years go by. For someone coming out of bankruptcy they should expect their scores to be back in the 600 range within two to three years if they do not have any further negative occurrences. To get the scores up faster it is important to reestablish credit as quickly as possible and be on-time with the payments, and watch balances on credit cards.

For someone with high scores it may take more effort to make the scores even higher. An example would be if you have credit cards established, but do not use them. Try using them for small purchases and paying the bill in full when it arrives. Keeping activity current can drive the scores higher. Of course the longer credit cards are open the higher the scores will go over time. Do not obsess too much over getting your scores to the 800 range. There is no further reward once your scores are over 740. The majority of the time, as long as you are over 720 you will always get the best terms available. However, striving to be higher ensures we have built up the fortress of positive credit that will offset anything negative that we may inadvertently encounter in the future. Do not lose sleep at night if your score is not at 800.

If you have a credit or mortgage related question or a story to share, you can email me at: Patrick@TheCreditRoadMap.com. I will do my best to respond to your questions and post them on my website at www.TheCreditRoadMap.com .

Appendix D: Example Letters

Dispute Letter To Credit Bureau

Name of Credit Bureau (*Equifax, TransUnion or Experian*):

Date:

To Whom It May Concern:

Please be advised that I have found information on the credit report you are providing to be inaccurate.

The following item(s) are incorrect:
(*Provide the name of the creditor(s), type of account, account number and line number from credit report if possible; describe what it is you are disputing about the account*)

I am requesting that the item be removed (*or request another specific change*) to correct the information.

Sincerely,

Your Name
Your DOB
Your Address
Your SSN

(You can get the most current address to mail disputes to by visiting the websites of the three credit bureaus: www.experian.com; www.transunion.com; www.equifax.com)

Request For Free Credit Report

Name of Credit Bureau (*Equifax, TransUnion or Experian*):

Date:

To Whom It May Concern:

Please be advised that I have been denied credit based on information contained in the report that you have provided. Please accept this as a request for a free copy of my credit report.

Enclosed is a copy of the denial letter from (*name of creditor*)

Sincerely,

Your Name
Your DOB
Your Address
Your SSN

(You can get the most current address to mail free report requests to by visiting the websites of the three credit bureaus: www.experian.com; www.transunion.com; www.equifax.com)

Identity Theft Notification to Credit Bureaus

Name of Credit Bureau (*Equifax, TransUnion or Experian*):

Date:

To Whom It May Concern:

Please be advised that I have been a victim of identity theft. This is my request for a fraud alert to be placed on my credit report and that I may receive a copy of my credit report for review.

Enclosed is a copy of the police report from (*name of agency*) regarding the nature of the identity theft.

Sincerely,

Your Name
Your DOB
Your Address
Your SSN

(You can get the most current address to mail ID theft notifications to by visiting the websites of the three credit bureaus: www.experian.com; www.transunion.com; www.equifax.com)

Validation of Debt Request

Name of Collection Agency:
Address
City, State, Zip
Date:
Re: Account #

To Whom It May Concern:

I received notification claiming that I owe a debt that is being collected by your company. Under Federal legislation, the Fair Debt Collection Practices Act, I am entitled to validation of said debt. Please forward evidence regarding the existence of the debt from the original creditor immediately.

This letter shall serve as notice that I am disputing the validity of the debt you claim I owe as no evidence has yet been provided. I have never inquired or received goods or services from your company, nor the company you represent.

I await your response to my request. If you are unable to provide proper documentation regarding the debt please forward me a statement showing zero balance owed.

Sincerely,

Your Name
Your DOB
Your Address

(Only send this if you genuinely believe you do not owe the debt, if you owe the debt make arrangements to pay it.)

Glossary of Terms

Account Review: A review of a consumer's credit history by existing creditors. Holders of revolving accounts will sometimes watch for negative changes in credit history that may result in the increase of interest rates or the decrease in available balances.

Accrued Interest: The amount of money to be repaid on a loan or note in addition to the amount originally borrowed.

Active Account: An account in which activity has been reported to a credit bureau in the past 90 days. An account that has not had activity in the past 90 days may have been paid in full or closed or may be inactive but remains open.

Adverse Credit: Negative information regarding a person's pattern of borrowing and repayment of debts as reported to the credit bureaus. Most commonly this will be late payments, past due amounts, collections, judgments, liens, etc.

Alias: A name reported in your credit file that differs from your primary or given name. This will occur if you apply for loans using variations of your name. An example would be: Kevin Smith or Kevin A. Smith Jr. This is common when someone is a Junior or a Senior, or when a last name changes due to marriage or divorce.

Amortization: The reduction of a loan debt through periodic installment payments of principal and interest. A loan amortized for five years would have payments (including principal and interest) that would reduce the balance until it was $0 at the end of the fifth year.

Annual Percentage Rate (APR): The yearly cost of the loan to the borrower. It reflects all finance charges, including interest and the costs to acquire the loan. Knowing the APR allows you to compare loans, even when they are structured differently. It shows the total cost of the loan to the consumer.

Asset: Any holding that has a monetary value. Real estate property, cars, jewelry, money in checking or savings, stocks, bonds, retirement accounts, etc. are all considered assets.

Authorized User: A person granted permission to sign for charges on a credit card by the primary user of that card. Authorized users are not legally responsible for payments, unlike a joint account. Being added as an authorized user can help the credit score as long as it is a positive account. Likewise it can damage the credit scores if the history is negative.

Available Credit: On a revolving account, the credit limit minus the current balance. The ratio between credit in use and the amount left available is a major factor in credit scoring. A 50% ratio should not be exceeded to avoid having a negative impact on credit scores. The lower the ratio, the better.

Balance: The outstanding amount owed to a creditor.

Balloon Payment: A final payment at the end of a loan term, which would be the amount remaining on the loan. Under most circumstances a borrower would refinance the amount into a new loan rather than pay off the full amount.

Bankruptcy: Discharge or arrangement for reduced payment of debt. Once a bankruptcy has been filed debt collection attempts automatically cease. It is a legally binding agreement made through the courts.

Borrower: Anyone who obtains funds from a lender in the form of a loan. The borrower is legally responsible for the repayment of the debt.

Capacity: An estimate of the amount of debt a borrower can handle in regards to the amount of income being earned and current existing debt. This is similar to debt-to-income ratio.

Capital: The amount of current assets, including savings, investments, and property. Similar to collateral or assets.

Chapter 7 Bankruptcy: The most common form of consumer bankruptcy. It typically releases a debtor from all liability for the debts included in a bankruptcy. However, not all debt is eligible for discharge in a bankruptcy (see Chapter 9). The debtor must forfeit personal property that was secured by any debt included in the bankruptcy. A Chapter 7 bankruptcy remains on the credit report for 10 years.

Chapter 11 Bankruptcy: Normally used by corporations, not by consumers.

Chapter 13 Bankruptcy: The debtor agrees to repay all or part of their debt over a period of time ranging from three to five years under most circumstances. The debtor will make a monthly payment that is more manageable than what their current monthly debt payment is. This is sometimes called a "Wage Earner Plan." The debtor will typically not have to forfeit personal property secured by debt. A Chapter 13 bankruptcy will remain on a credit report for seven years.

Character: A measure of how one approaches the responsibility of repaying debt. This is measured by a consumer's credit history and resulting credit score. This is something given very strong consideration in making a lending decision.

Charge Card: A credit card that requires full payment of the balance each month. American Express is an example of such a card. On the credit report the current balance shows up as the payment amount due.

Charge-off: A situation in which a borrower is seriously delinquent in paying a bill. For accounting purposes the creditor lists the debt as "bad" or "uncollectible." Once an account goes to charge-off it will be sent to a collection agency in an attempt to recoup the debt partially or in whole. Many people mistakenly think a charge-off means the original creditor is no longer pursuing the debt and therefore nothing is owed. This is not the case.

Closed Account: An account that has been closed by either the borrower or creditor. A balance could still be owed on a closed revolving account; however, no new charges may be made to the account. A creditor will typically close a revolving account if it becomes excessively or frequently past due. Closed accounts can remain on your credit report for seven years from the date of last activity. When an account is closed it does not erase the history from factoring into the credit scores. Many people mistakenly assume late payments will go away by closing an account, which is false.

Closing: The point at which the buyer signs their mortgage documents, pays closing costs and down payment, and becomes the owner of the property. This is the point in the loan process where the loan documents are official and copies should be placed in a safe place. Copies of final loan documents may be necessary to prove any errors in loan terms or for a future refinance of the loan. Closing is also known as settlement.

Closing Costs: Expenses associated in acquiring a new loan or mortgage. Closing costs may include points, origination fees, underwriting and processing fees, title/attorney fees, and other costs.

Collateral: Property that acts as security for the repayment of a loan. If the loan is not repaid the property will be repossessed or foreclosed upon. Often collateral will be a house or a car, but it is not limited to these items.

Collection Agency: A firm assigned by an original creditor to collect unpaid or overdue amounts from a loan or service.

Consolidation Loan: A loan obtained in order to combine multiple debts into one. This is very common for student loans.

Consumer Debt: Money owed on loans through credit cards and car loans. Based on the idea of consumption, something that has no return of value. Different from mortgages and student loans which can provide a valuable return on the money borrowed.

Consumer Credit Counseling (CCC): Organizations that help consumers find a way to repay debts through budgeting and money management. Typically a non-profit entity, but this is not always the case. Consumer Credit Counseling is considered an alternative to bankruptcy.

Consumer Reporting Agency: A company that reports consumer credit history in regards to specific account payments, balances, etc. Also known as Credit Bureau.

Co-signer: A borrower who signs on a loan with another party and becomes equally liable for the repayment of the debt. The debt will appear on the credit report of a co-signer.

Convenience Checks: A check linked to a credit card account. They can be used for balance transfers or to make purchases.

Credit Bureau: A company that reports consumer credit history in regards to specific account payments, balances, etc. The bureaus receive, maintain, and provide credit information on consumers. There are three major credit bureaus: Experian, Equifax, and TransUnion. There are smaller companies that act as credit bureaus, but most are regional arms of the three major bureaus. Also known as a Consumer Reporting Agency.

Credit Card: A card attached to a revolving account. It is used to make purchases and can also be used to gain cash advances. Credit cards typically have a minimum payment due each month that is 3% - 4% of the outstanding balance.

Credit Card Issuer: A bank or other lending institution that extends revolving credit through an issued credit card.

Credit File: An individual's credit history, identifying information, and other records maintained as a record by a credit reporting company. The credit file is the source from which a credit report is generated.

Credit Fraud/Identity Theft: A crime involving the use of another person's identity to gain credit or make purchases. This could either be the theft of an existing credit card or the creation of a new account under a false pretense. The criminal will often steal names, addresses, account numbers and social security numbers to commit the crime.

Credit History: A record of past performance in the repaying of debt. Lenders use this as a guide to determining the likelihood of a borrower making payments on-time. The credit report shows a complete credit history, which is a major factor in how credit scores are calculated.

Credit Limit/Credit Line: The amount of available credit issued by a lender. A borrower may not exceed the available amount given by the lender.

Credit Repair Agencies/Credit Clinics: These companies may claim to be able to "erase bad debts" under any circumstance. Such entities charge a wide range of fees to attempt the clean up of a credit report.

Credit Report: A report generated based on the credit history of a consumer contained in the credit file with the credit bureaus. Prospective lenders use the report as a tool in making a lending decision based on what habits are reflected in the report (i.e. on-time payment, good management of debts, etc.). The credit report is a complete history of all accounts that have been reported by creditors.

Credit Risk: The likelihood of a consumer to repay an outstanding debt on-time. Lenders assesses credit risk in making a lending decision.

Credit Score: A numerical estimation of the likelihood that a consumer will repay a debt on-time. The most commonly used scoring model was created by Fair Isaac, and is often referred to as a FICO® score. Variations of the model are used across the industry by the credit bureaus. Credit scores are often used in generating automated approvals of loans for consumers.

Creditor: Any person who offers or extends credit creating a debt or to whom a debt is owed. Also known as lender. Responsible for receiving payments, maintaining the account, and correctly reporting the account history to the credit bureaus.

Creditworthiness: An assessment of a consumer's past credit history, which is a strong indication of future behavior. A lender will use this assessment to determine whether or not to extend credit to a consumer.

Daily Periodic Rate: The annual percentage rate of a credit card divided by 365 days.

Debt-to-Income Ratio: A calculation of monthly debts to monthly income. Lenders use this calculation in making lending decisions. The lower the ratio the better it looks in the eyes of a lender.

Default: When a borrower consistently fails to make payments; failure to fulfill an agreed-upon financial obligation. Once classified as being in default it is assumed the debt will not be repaid.

Deferment: When a loan is in a period of time that does not require repayment. This is typical for student loans when a student borrower is a full-time student or has just graduated.

Delinquent: When a debt has become overdue. Once payment has not been received by the due date it is now delinquent or late. In order for a delinquency to be reported to the credit bureaus it must be 30 days past the due date.

Discharge: The release of a debtor from responsibility for a debt. This is most commonly associated with a Chapter 7 bankruptcy.

Disclosure Statement: A form that details to a borrower the terms of a loan and outlines repayment.

Discretionary Income: The money left over when all expenses and other financial obligations have been paid.

Dismissed Bankruptcy: When a judge rules against the petition of bankruptcy. The discharge of the debt has been denied and the filer still legally owes on the debt. In the public records section of the credit report it will show the bankruptcy status as dismissed.

Down Payment: A percentage of the total purchase price paid initially to establish a loan on a purchase. A larger down payment will often coincide with better terms on the interest rate for the amount borrowed.

Electronic Funds Transfer (EFT): The electronic transfer of loan proceeds from a lender to a borrower or third party intermediary.

Fannie Mae: A congressionally chartered secondary-mortgage market company that buys loans from private lenders. It is a private, shareholder-owned company that works to make sure mortgage money is available for people in communities all across America. Fannie Mae sets precedence when it comes to mortgage underwriting guidelines to assure end investors on Wall Street that the investments being made are safe. Fannie Mae is similar to Freddie Mac in the sense that both entities have the same congressional charter. The two were formed to create competition in the secondary-mortgage market.

FICO® Score: The brand name of the most widely used credit scoring model in the industry.

Finance Charge: The cost of a loan expressed as a dollar amount.

Fixed Rate: An interest rate that remains the same for the life of the loan. A fixed rate allows someone to budget for a specific payment because the principal and interest payment will remain the same.

Forbearance: The temporary postponement of payments due to varying circumstances, but most often times financial hardship. Forbearance is a good solution for someone who is unable to make payments on their student loans. It keeps payments from becoming late and therefore will keep the credit scores from suffering. In some cases it may be possible to back date a forbearance to a date prior to when payments became late.

Foreclosure: The legal proceeding by which a creditor/lien holder may sell mortgaged property to recover a defaulted debt. A mortgage debt is secured by the property, failure to make payments will result in the property being taken back by the bank to be sold. Once a mortgage payment is 120 days past due it will typically be considered in foreclosure.

Fraud Alert: Notification to the credit bureaus that a consumer makes when there is suspicion of identity theft or credit fraud. The credit report will show that a fraud alert is in place. The fraud alert will make lenders aware of the possibility that the person applying for a loan or credit card could be an identity thief.

Freddie Mac: A congressionally chartered secondary-mortgage market company that buys loans from private lenders. It is a private, shareholder-owned company that works to make sure mortgage money is available for people in communities all across America. Freddie Mac sets precedence when it comes to mortgage underwriting guidelines to assure end investors on Wall Street that the investments being made are safe. Freddie Mac is similar to Fannie Mae in the sense that both entities have the same congressional charter. The two were formed to create competition in the secondary-mortgage market.

Garnishment: A legal process whereby a creditor is able to receive a specified sum from wages earned by a debtor to make payment toward satisfying a judgment.

Grace Period: A period of time between when a charge is made on a credit card and when it becomes due or starts accumulating interest. Can also be a period of time after graduation before a student loan requires repayment.

Gross Monthly Income: Wages earned before taxes are deducted. Gross income is used when qualifying for a mortgage.

Guarantee: A commitment by the guarantor to reimburse a lender or subsequent holder of an approved loan when the borrower fails to repay the loan due to the borrower's death, disability, default, or bankruptcy. This is common with loans that are "backed" by the government such as mortgages (FHA, VA, and USDA) and student loans.

Hard Inquiry: An indication that a consumer has applied for a loan. In the credit report it shows a listing of all pulls of the credit for at least the past 90 days, who pulled it and what date it was pulled.

Home Equity: The part of your home you own, or the home's current appraised value minus the amount you still owe. Home equity is built by making principal payments or by appreciation in value.

Home Equity Loan: A loan secured by available equity on a property. Typically falling in the category of a second mortgage as it follows lien position to the first mortgage. A second mortgage, like a first mortgage, can go into foreclosure if the payments are not made.

Identity Theft: A crime involving the use of another person's identity to gain credit or make purchases. This could either be the theft of an existing credit card or the creation of a new account under a false pretense. The criminal will often steal names, addresses, account numbers and social security numbers to commit the crime.

Incomplete Loan: A loan application submitted where some or all of the necessary documentation has not been received. At this state it is not approved or denied, although denial could occur if the required documentation is not received in a certain period of time.

Index: An index is a money market rate such as the prime rate, treasury bill, or LIBOR that lenders use to determine interest rates for the loans they offer to customers. An index is used almost exclusively for variable rate loans and is typically combined with a margin.

Inquiry: An instance in which all or part of your credit file is accessed by a company or individual. Inquiries stay on your credit report for no more than two years. There are various types of inquiries such as hard, soft, or promotional.

Installment Loan: A credit account in which the amount of the payment and the number of payments are predetermined or fixed. Being late on an installment loan is worse than being late on a revolving account.

Interest: A charge or cost to a borrower for use of a lender's money. The cost of borrowing, usually expressed in a percentage rate.

Interest Rate: The actual rate of simple interest paid by the borrower. The amount charged by a lender for borrowing money. Different types include: 1. Variable: Will adjust according to economic and market conditions. This could be monthly, or annually. 2. Fixed: The interest rate will remain the same for the entire term of the loan.

Joint Account: A credit or loan account held by two or more people. All account holders assume legal responsibility for the repayment of the account. The account shows up on the credit reports of all borrowers on the account.

Joint Credit Report: A combined report created by merging the credit files of joint applicants and used by creditors to assess a joint application for credit, typically used with married co-borrowers. The credit files remain separate; a joint credit report does not join or mix credit accounts.

Judgment: The requirement of a person to fulfill an obligation as determined in a court of law by a judge or referee. In terms of credit we are typically talking about small claims court. Judgments would appear in the public records section of the credit report where bankruptcy and tax liens would appear.

Late Charges: Charges that a lender may require the borrower to pay if the borrower fails to pay all or a portion of a required installment or minimum payment by the due date. Some loans allow for a period of days after the due date before a late penalty would be assessed. In the case of most mortgages it is due on the 1st of the month, but is not late unless received after the 15th of the month. Also known as a late fee.

Late Payment: A payment delivered after its due date. Payments that are late by 30 days or more will likely be reported to the credit bureaus and added to your credit report. Late payments are the quickest way to ruin a credit score. There is a hierarchy of late payments that goes 30, 60, 90, 120, etc. Once an account reaches 120 days without payment it is considered in default and is unlikely to be paid without collection procedures.

Lease: A contract that allows you the right to use or occupy property (a car or apartment, for example) over a specific length of time, during which you make regular payments and after which you do not own the property. A car lease is typically contained on the credit report just like a car loan would be. Leased property will not typically report on a credit report unless it is not paid and goes to collection or judgment.

Lender: An entity that lends money to consumers or enables them to make purchases by extending credit. Also known as a creditor.

Liability: The responsibility of repayment of borrowed funds. It can be looked at in monthly terms when calculating monthly debt or in overall terms when assessing all outstanding debt amounts.

Lien: A legal claim upon real or personal property as security for or payment of a debt. This can vary from a mortgage (which is a lien against a property), to a tax lien from the government, to a mechanics lien from a contractor who was not paid. The latter two would be negative items on the credit report.

Line of Credit: 1) A credit limit established by a creditor as the maximum that may be borrowed for an account. 2) A second mortgage set up as a revolving account with a variable rate.

Loan: An extension of money that is to be repaid over a specified period of time with monthly payments.

Loan-to-Value Ratio (LTV): The ratio of the amount of a home loan to the appraised value of the home. For example, if you borrow $150,000 to buy a $200,000 house, the LTV is 75%.

Merged Credit Report: A credit report that contains information from all three of the major credit bureaus (Experian, Equifax, and TransUnion). Lenders will use the middle of the three scores as the actual credit score. This is also known as a tri-merge report.

Minimum Payment: The required amount of monthly payment on a revolving credit card account. It is generally 2% - 5% of the balance.

Mortgage: A loan that facilitates the purchase of a home, the home itself serves as collateral for the loan.

Net Income: Total income from employment and other sources, minus taxes. Banks typically consider gross income in qualifying.

Obsolete Information: Information that comes off of a credit report at a specified period of time. A late payment from over seven years ago would be considered obsolete and would need to come off of the credit report.

Origination Fee: A fee charged to consumers as a closing cost to borrow funds. An origination will often equal 1% of the loan amount. It is also known as a "point."

Periodic Rate: An interest rate expressed in daily or monthly terms. It is calculated by dividing the annual percentage rate (APR) by 365 or by 12.

PITI: An acronym representing the main components of a monthly mortgage payment: principal, interest, taxes, and insurance.

Points: Charges levied by a mortgage lender, also known as origination or discount. One point equals 1% of the value of the loan.

Pre-Approval: When an applicant's credit has been pulled and enough information has been verified to give approval based on the current circumstances. In the case of a mortgage, many people get pre-approved prior to looking for a house. In doing this they know what they qualify for and are not looking at houses they can not afford. A contract, appraisal, clear title, and other details on the house would need to be completed before a full approval could be made.

Primary User: The person under whose name a credit card account is listed. A primary user can authorize other people to use the account. The primary user is responsible for making the payments on the debt.

Prime Rate: The rate at which banks borrow money from each other. Prime rate is an index used by variable-rate loan programs such as home equity lines of credit.

Principal: 1) The amount paid that reduces the balance each month. 2) The balance of the amount borrowed minus interest and other charges.

Principal Balance: The outstanding amount of the loan on which interest is charged.

Promissory Note: The legally binding document or "promise to pay" that a borrower signs before receiving loan proceeds. The promissory note includes information outlining the terms and conditions of the loan.

Promotional Inquiry: When a person's credit meets the criteria of a targeted direct mail campaign. Limited information is available such as your name, address, and possibly a range of your credit score. A full credit report or credit pull is not involved. Opting out will keep promotional inquiries from taking place.

Public Record: Information obtained from court records / county recorders about things such as state or federal tax liens, bankruptcy, and judgments in civil actions.

Qualifying Ratio: The ratio of your monthly expenses to your gross monthly income. Same as debt-to-income ratio.

Refinancing: Replacing an existing mortgage with a new mortgage on the same property to either lower interest, pull out cash from equity, or remove a borrower from the original mortgage.

Repayment Period: The period during which interest accrues on the loan and principal payments are required.

Repossession: The act of a creditor regaining possession of an item that was collateral on a loan.

Revolving Balance: The balance on a credit card. Unlike an installment loan balance, it can go up or down from month to month and has no set period of when it will be paid in full.

Satisfied: The status given to a judgment once payment has been made. On a credit report if a judgment is not reporting as satisfied it is assumed the debt is still owed (typically it will say "not satisfied" or "unknown").

Second Mortgage: A mortgage taken out on a home that has an existing 1st mortgage in place. The second mortgage assumes a greater risk as the second lien holder. If the house were to be foreclosed and sold, the 1st mortgage holder would be paid all money owed before the second mortgage holder would be paid anything toward what is owed on the second mortgage. Since there is greater risk on second mortgages, the rates are generally higher than what a 1st mortgage would offer.

Secured Credit Card: A credit card secured by a savings account or some other form of deposit to act as collateral against charges made. These types of cards can come with heavier costs than traditional credit cards. However, these types of cards are useful in building or reestablishing credit.

Secured Loan: A loan for which an item of property has been pledged in case of default. A mortgage or car loan is an example of a secured loan, because the house or car would be taken back if the loan is not paid.

Security: Collateral that acts as an exchange if a loan is not repaid. It is a physical piece of property that will guarantee a loan's repayment.

Service Charge: A fee charged in connection to a loan.

Servicer: An entity that maintains and collects monthly payments of accounts. A loan could be originated by one lender, but sold to a different lender for servicing. This is very common in the mortgage industry.

Settlement: Closing of a transaction.

Social Security Number (SSN): The unique nine-digit number assigned to every legal resident of the United States by the Social Security Administration. Because no two people are assigned the same number, the SSN is usually the main identifying factor in a person's records, including credit reports.

Soft Inquiry: When your credit report is accessed without affecting your credit rating. Soft inquiries include your own requests for your credit report or when an existing creditor checks on your credit history.

Sub-prime: A term for the financial market regarding consumers with low credit scores. A high risk class of financing that generally results in higher interest rates and worse terms than consumers with good credit.

Tax Lien: A charge upon real or personal property for the satisfaction of debts related to unpaid taxes. A tax lien will show up on the credit report for seven years after the date it was paid.

Three-in-one Credit Report: A comprehensive credit report containing credit information from all three of the major credit reporting companies. See Merged Credit Report.

Tradeline: A credit industry term for an account listed on a credit report. Each account reported to the credit bureaus is a separate tradeline.

Treasury Bill Rate (T-bill Rate): The rate paid by the government on its short-term borrowing. The rate is reset periodically. Treasury Bill rates are indexes used by variable-rate loan programs

Tri-Merge Credit Report: See Merged Credit Report.

Unsecured Loan: A loan based on your promise to repay, not on pledged collateral.

Vacated: A judgment that has been dismissed or reversed from a previous ruling of the court. An action that makes the original judgment legally void.

Variable Interest Rate: An interest rate that can change/adjust over the course of time the loan is outstanding. It will change according to an index which is an economic indicator such as the prime rate, treasury bill, or LIBOR to name a few.

Wage Earner Plan: A name for a Chapter 13 bankruptcy. Under this plan a debtor would repay a portion of the debts owed until full payment has been received.

Resources

Annual Credit Report:	www.annualcreditreport.com
American Bankruptcy Institute:	www.abiworld.org
Credit Center at LAWDOG®:	www.lawdog.com/credit.htm
Equifax:	www.equifax.com
Experian:	www.experian.com
Federal Citizen Information Center:	www.pueblo.gsa.gov
Federal Deposit Insurance Corporation:	www.fdic.gov
Federal Reserve:	www.federalreserve.gov
Federal Trade Commission:	www.ftc.gov
FICO:	www.myfico.com
Identity Theft:	www.consumer.gov/idtheft www.idtheftcenter.org
Jump$tart Coalition for Personal Financial Literacy:	www.jumpstart.org
Legal Information Institute of the Cornell Law School:	www.law.cornell.edu
MasterCard:	www.mastercardintl.com
National Association of Attorneys General:	www.naag.org

National Consumer Law Center:	www.consumerlaw.org
Office of the Comptroller of the Currency:	www.occ.treas.gov
Public Interest Research Group:	www.pirg.org
Social Security Agency:	www.ssa.gov
The National Credit Reporting Association, Inc:	www.ncrainc.org
TransUnion:	www.transunion.com
U.S. Bankruptcy Courts:	www.uscourts.gov/bankruptcy courts.html
U.S. Department of Housing and Urban Development:	www.hud.gov
U.S. Financial Literacy and Education Commission:	www.mymoney.gov
Visa:	www.visa.com

Index

consolidating, 39

consolidation loan, 199

consumer credit counseling (CCC), 126, 130-131, 135, 137, 141-144, 182, 201

Consumer Credit Protection Act of 1968, 175

consumer debt, 138, 199

Consumer Federation of America (CFA), 109

consumer reporting agency, 52, 177, 200

consumers, 4, 9-10, 17-18, 20, 22, 26, 28-32, 34, 40, 42-44, 49, 52-55, 58, 63-65, 67, 72, 75, 78, 80-83, 85, 87-88, 109, 115-117, 122, 124, 126-127, 129-132, 136-144, 150-151, 153, 157, 160, 168-169, 174-179, 186, 188, 196, 198-202, 204-207, 209, 212, 214-215, 217-219

conventional mortgage, 170

co-signer, 65, 106, 151-152, 154, 200

co-signing, 105-106, 185

convenience checks, 200

credit applications, 117

credit bureaus, 32, 34, 36, 41, 49-55, 57-60, 68, 70, 72, 78-79, 81-82, 85, 87-88, 114, 116-117, 121-122, 124-125, 129, 133-134, 145, 151, 153, 164-166, 177, 180-182, 184-185, 188, 193-195, 197, 201-203, 205, 208-209, 213

credit cards, 20-22, 29, 36-48, 50, 56, 61, 66, 73, 77, 80, 86-87, 90-92, 98, 100-105, 110-112, 115, 117-118, 122-124, 126-128, 134-138, 146-147, 151-154, 156, 159-160, 165-166, 176, 182, 184-187, 189-190, 197-202, 204-205, 208-211

credit card issuer, 47, 200

credit counseling, 126, 130-131, 135, 137, 141-144, 182, 201

credit file, 67, 75, 89, 99, 132-133, 196, 200-201, 206

credit history, 30, 33, 36, 38, 40, 46, 51, 69, 76, 84, 91, 115-116, 119, 139, 146-151, 153, 196, 198, 200-202, 212

The Credit Jungle, 46

credit limits, 15, 20, 37, 44, 70, 92, 100, 111, 153, 180, 186, 197, 201, 208

credit monitoring, 80

credit repair, 131-134, 152, 201

credit reports, 9, 13, 18, 26, 28-38, 41-43, 46-60, 62-72, 74-81, 83-84, 86-88, 90-93, 95, 97-99, 101, 103, 105, 112, 114-120, 122-129, 132, 134, 137-138, 140, 142, 146-148, 150, 155, 163-164, 167, 172, 177, 179-181, 183-184, 186-187, 189-190, 192-194, 198-201, 203-208, 210-212, 215

credit risk, 201

credit scores, 11, 26-31, 34-46, 54, 58, 62, 64, 69, 74, 76-79, 86, 91-93, 103-105, 114-120, 134, 138, 147, 150, 152, 168-173, 179-180, 182, 184, 188-189, 197, 199, 201, 204, 212

non-profit, 130, 142, 163, 201

sub-prime, 75, 213
T
tax lien, 33, 47, 49, 62, 143, 184, 208-209, 211, 213
telephone, 18, 31, 44, 64-65, 72, 79-80, 95, 149, 151, 153-154
Texas Automobile Dealers Association, 28
thin file, 145
three-in-one credit report, 213
time frame, 42, 137
timeshare, 99
tradeline, 41, 127, 147, 213
trademark laws, 23
traditional credit, 46, 150-152, 212
TransUnion, 31,33, 55, 58, 79, 193-195, 201, 209, 216
treasury bill rate, 207, 213
tri-merge credit report, 31, 55, 209, 213
Truth in Lending Act (TILA), 179
U
unfair, 17, 26, 178
Uniform Retail Credit Classification and Account Management Policy, 122
universal default, 44
unpaid, 49, 93, 99, 104, 129, 200, 213
unsecured, 117, 126, 154, 166, 213
U.S. Government Accountability Office, 18
U.S. Public Interest Research Group, 69
USA Today, 9, 20-21
U.S.D.A. Rural Housing, 190
V
VA, 149, 170, 190, 206
vacate, 49, 213
variable interest rate, 207, 209, 213
Veterans Affairs (VA), 149, 170, 190, 206
Visa, 20, 22, 136, 216
W
wage earner plan, 140, 144, 199, 214
The Wall Street Journal, 23
wallet, 22, 45, 56, 157, 160
Western Union, 162
Z
Zagorsky, Jay, 100

Ordering Information

Bulk Order Chart for *The Credit Road Map*

5-10 Books	$20 each
11-20 Books	$17 each
21-40 Books	$15 each
41-100 Books	$14 each
101-999 Books	$12 each
1,000+ Books	$11 each

To place a bulk order, email Info@TheCreditRoadMap.com or call 480-219-3010.

A DVD of a class Patrick presented based on *The Credit Road Map* is available at www.TheCreditRoadMap.com.

Visit www.TheCreditRoadMap.com for free articles and downloads of useful manuals.

To book Patrick Ritchie to speak to your organization about credit please email Bookings@TheCreditRoadMap.com or call 480-219-3010.

If you are interested in attending a class in your area please email Classes@TheCreditRoadMap.com to be notified when a class will be held in your city or state.